D1357004

Historians I Have Known

HISTORIANS
I HAVE KNOWN

A.L. Rowse

*Good historians are the
most scarce of all writers.*
Horace Walpole

Duckworth

First published in 1995 by
Gerald Duckworth & Co. Ltd.
The Old Piano Factory
48 Hoxton Square, London N1 6PB
Tel: 0171 729 5986
Fax: 0171 729 0015

A catalogue record for this book is available
from the British Library

ISBN 0 7156 2649 3

Photoset in North Wales by
Derek Doyle & Associates, Mold, Clwyd
Printed in Great Britain by
Biddles Ltd, Guildford and King's Lynn

Contents

To
Roger Makins
(Lord Sherfield)
to recall
tutorials at Christ Church long ago

Preface

Once again I was indebted to Colin Haycraft, scholar and publisher, for suggesting to me a subject I should not otherwise have thought of. The roll-call here is naturally weighted on the side of Oxford, for there I spent most of my long working life. This does not mean that I have not been acquainted with many more figures in the profession elsewhere. I place at the head two who were not only great historians but great men – G.M. Trevelyan of Cambridge and Samuel Eliot Morison of Harvard. It was an honour to be welcomed into their confidence as their friend. The accent throughout is from personal acquaintance, as I was instructed.

After the war I was invited to edit a large series, *Teach Yourself History* (now *Men and their Times*). For this I wrote an introductory volume, *The Use of History*, of which the American edition, revised for paperback, is the more up-to-date text. The *utility* of history was at that time strikingly obvious, with a practising historian as our leader in Churchill. He knew what to expect of Germany from her record in the past century – as against Chamberlain, who knew no history and neither Germany nor Europe. It is a necessity to know something – and the more the better – of a country's past form in dealing with it. Catherine the Great, of Russia, said revealingly that Russia was 'ungovernable'. Looking at French history one sees that the French like autocratic government based on popular acclaim: hence the Bonapartes, Napoleon III, and de Gaulle. One has a clue to the difficulties of American government in the division of powers between President and Congress, built into the Constitution by the Founding Fathers.

At home it is no less obvious that, if one is to be a good leader in the community, in the civil service, local social services, in

vii

education, in the forces, especially the historic Royal Navy and Army, one needs a proper apprenticeship, learning how things have come to be as they are, a useful knowledge of the past.

Yet this is not what has held me to history, as with poetry, all my life. They are analogous, partners – I may say shortly, the *poetry* of history, as Trevelyan saw. Strangely enough, few historians have been poets (though Macaulay was) – perhaps they found the poetry in history sufficient, as certainly Froude, Powicke and David Knowles did. I realised that McFarlane did, though he was too inhibited to express it.

For myself, I *love* research. The historian always wants to *know*. So I suppose I was meant to be an historian from the time I was a boy, getting into trouble for being 'inquisitive'. If I had not been irrepressibly inquisitive I should never have settled the problems of Shakespeare's autobiography in the Sonnets, or discovered the identity of the Dark Lady, the remarkable half-Italian young woman, poet and feminist, with whom he was infatuated in those years. To solve these problems firmly needed firm dating and chronology – hence an Elizabethan historian was indispensable.

More largely, it stands to reason that for full appreciation of Shakespeare's work one needs a good knowledge of the age and time in which he lived, of which his work gives the fullest expression. It is absurd – and intellectually second-rate – to think that one can do without it. It is a merely temporary aberration of literary scholars to think that history throws no light on their work. Their loss! History and literature go together. The best historians make the fullest use of literature.

Think too of the *pleasures* of our subject. It adds a whole dimension to our enjoyment of life, what we see in the landscape, going round the country, the buildings in an old country, medieval or Tudor, Georgian or Victorian. An American art-historian commented to me what an advantage we enjoy, growing up naturally among them, whereas in a new country they have to learn them like a new language. Still, even in the United States one finds the character and elegance of New England or Southern Colonial, the historicity and pathos of the old Spanish missions, more eloquent and appealing than the rigid skyscrapers.

Preface

Enough. Sir John Neale said of *The Use of History* that it was a 'generous' book. I hope that this successor – though it must not be uncritical in its estimates and judgements – may come also, by and large, under that heading.

Spring 1995   A.L.R.

CHAPTER 1

G.M. Trevelyan

Trevelyan was the head of our profession in his time, and behaved as such. He was markedly an *encourager* of other people's work, not a *dis*courager, as lesser mortals are apt to be. He once said to me, of his Cambridge medievalists, that he felt that they were engaged in looking over each other's shoulders. I agreed that academics were apt to sting each other into frustration (like my old friend McFarlane).

Trevelyan was made in a bigger, more old-fashioned mould. With that tremendous background – an eminent historian, Sir George Otto Trevelyan, for father, Macaulay for great-uncle – George Macaulay Trevelyan sat on Olympus. He didn't mind the criticism of inferiors, he hardly seemed to notice them. This was a great strength, and – my goodness – what he achieved!

He was researching and writing all the time. This obsessiveness is characteristic of genius – though he would not have it to be. Conventional, though genuine, modesty – upper-class self-deprecation – all the same, I regard him as having genius, and was not persuaded by his denial.

What were his qualities?

A passion for landscape and topography with a flair for describing it, absolute honesty, transparent candour and fairness of mind; constructive power witnessed to intellect – all *his* books had structure; wide and comprehending common sense, to an uncommon degree; dedication to research and finding out the truth about things, hence to *understand* the past. Then, on top of all and beneath all was the poetry, the sense of mystery in the apprehension of dead men's lives by those yet alive.

It may surprise people in a professor, but to him 'its chief but not only value is poetic. Its poetic value depended upon its being a true record of actual happenings in the past. For the mystery of time past continually enthralls me.'

The relation of history to poetry is very subtle; one cannot quite get to the bottom of it. But the writing of history and the writing of poetry are not antithetical, as some people think, though very rare – witness Macaulay, Scott, Samuel Daniel. For Trevelyan poetry stood in place of religion, or was a kind of religion. All his life long he absorbed poetry. He knew all Macaulay's *Lays* by heart – 'Turn me on anywhere' – and hundreds of other verses, particularly Meredith's. (Revealing – and here a difference: I cannot like Meredith, with his forced optimism, Hardy is my man.) When Trevelyan grew old, half blind, and couldn't read, he consoled himself by reciting the poetry he knew. His last book was a literary one, *A Layman's Love of Letters*, notably approved by Eliot. No conflict beween history and poetry.

In his last history book he wrote, 'There is nothing that more divides civilised from semi-savage man than to be conscious of our forefathers as they really were, and bit by bit to reconstruct the mosaic of the long forgotten past ... How far can we know the real life of men in each successive age of the past?' he asks. The answer: 'It is only by study that we can see our forerunners, remote and recent, in their habits as they lived, intent each on the business of a long-vanished day, riding out to do homage or to poll a vote; to seize a neighbour's manor-house and carry off his ward, or to leave cards on ladies in crinolines.'

We see that he was a romantic (as Namier was not). His feeling for history was so living that it was practically contemporary. I was much amused when he said one day, about the younger Pitt's repressive legislation against the Corresponding Societies propaganding on behalf of the French Revolution, 'Billy Pitt, damn his eyes!' There was the old Radical, it might be Charles James Fox speaking. I, of course, disagreed: I said that Pitt had to keep order in the nursery. Trevelyan welcomed disagreement, and relished argument. His sympathies were so wide as to encompass rebels. Mine not: any fool can criticise and oppose, but can he do the job of government? To see the problems and responsibilities of government is a more mature business than to be forever on your hind legs calling everything in question.

One day he astonished me by speaking up for a Jacobite rebel, the last Earl of Derwentwater, coming out in the forlorn hope of the Rebellion of 1715. What? Ruin his family for a most hopeless cause? Well, the old boy was in favour of his taking a chance. Goodness, there was no such chance, only wreck and ruin stared the fool in the face – and I have never indulged in sympathy for foolery in human affairs, bringing down only more suffering upon hapless humans. Trevelyan approved of the use of moral disapproval in writing history. Very well, then ... expose foolery – whether James II's or his rebels'.

We had an argument about a crucial issue here. Would I have signed the letter inviting William of Orange to invade and put things right in 1688? Of course I approved of it – but I would not have signed it. At that Trevelyan bridled: 'Why not?' 'Because I don't sufficiently trust people.' It was his turn to be shocked: 'I think the less of you for that.'

Never mind: it was a difference not only of temperament and conviction, but of generation. Trevelyan was a Victorian, to him things were straight, he had no scepticism whatever. I don't think he understood, certainly he would not have approved, my combination of scepticism and aestheticism – fundamentally in line with Burckhardt. Trevelyan's tastes were Victorian. He had lived much of his life in Northumberland without ever going to see Vanbrugh's masterpiece there, Seaton Delaval. I persuaded him to go over. He didn't like it. The Victorians couldn't bear Blenheim Palace.

Anyone intelligent living through the experiences of our time could never enjoy the happy security of the Victorians, or the innocence of their moral standards. Trevelyan was in for his share of disillusionment, but would stand up for his heroes. John Bright now, the pacifist Quaker Radical, whose biography he had written – I said I had not read the book, he was *not* my cup of tea. Trevelyan put me right: 'You may not like him, but he helped largely to keep us out of the American Civil War.' That was a strong point in his favour, though I do not think that Britain could have intervened anyhow.

He did not hold with my bias against the Puritans. Naturally not – Victorians were much too biased in their favour. He simply said that, if it had not been for their spirit, we should not have contended with the Armada. I replied that, if it had not been for the extremists on the other side, we should not have needed to. I detested the extremists on *both* sides making life intolerable for sensible people in the middle.

I don't think he cared for this Laodicean, neutral position, and he clearly did not assess the destruction such people wrought in both the sixteenth and seventeenth centuries. That was what I minded most. In the hideous French Wars of Religion my position was that of the moderates, the clever and humane *politiques*, Montaigne and Michel de L'Hôpital. Or, in England, with Elizabeth I and Shakespeare.

Anyhow, he thought there was a place for some bias in history.

Once we had a set-to about Baldwin. Trevelyan, like so many, had been seduced by his private charm – he was at least an educated reading man, Trinity and all. I urged the shocking irresponsibility of his taking no interest in foreign affairs – with Mussolini and Hitler on the rampage, and Dover only twenty miles across from the Continent!

With utter honesty Trevelyan met me half-way and put the only consideration on Baldwin's behalf. 'You may well be right. All I will say is that it is difficult for a man to be equally good on home *and* foreign affairs.' That was the case of Sir Robert Walpole, best man on home affairs, brought down on foreign policy. Trevelyan did not have the meanness, as Tories did afterwards, to blame the catastrophe on Labour's stupid opposition to Rearmament. The Party was in a hopeless minority all the time: it was the duty of government to warn the country of its danger, and to *lead*, not follow.

Disillusionment hit Trevelyan worst over his beloved Italy, which he knew well – he had served in the British Ambulance Corps throughout the war on the Italian Front. 'I got to love the unadulterated Italian people of all time, a lovable people whom that wretch tried to bully and drill into second-rate Germans – and failed.' So much for Mussolini.

This remained a continuing grief to Trevelyan, for he had made his name and fame with his three Garibaldi books, especially the first, *Garibaldi's Defence of the Roman Republic*, which he wrote in a white heat of inspiration. Trevelyan got to know every mile of the ground Garibaldi fought over, in this and his later campaigns. A tremendous walker – he could do forty miles a day with ease – he walked all over it, in Sicily too. He fell in love with the charm of the Italian people, and thought, rather simply, of Mussolini as betraying them. He omitted to note, Liberal as he was, that there was *that* element in their character too – Mussolini played on it, and Italian Liberals handed it to him on a plate.

In later disenchantment Trevelyan charged his book with 'reeking' with bias. That was too strong a condemnation again. The fact was that he liked a simple heroic type like Garibaldi. He admitted that he had not understood the dilemmas of French policy, nor the exigencies of the position of the Papacy. The unification of Italy was inevitable in some form, and Cavour was the man to bring it about. My sympathies were with the politic, and devious, Cavour, not with simple types like Garibaldi and Mazzini.

I confess that when later I read the books of my old Christ Church friend, Harold Acton, on the Medicis of Florence and the Bourbons of Naples, I felt something of his sympathy for the Ancien Régime; I did not share any enthusiasm for the bourgeois Risorgimento. Trevelyan made a marked distinction between Sicilians and Italians of the mainland, and pointed out an open rift here – namely that, in supporting Garibaldi, Sicilians mistakenly thought that he was liberating them from the rule of the mainland. Sicilian writers, such as Verga, Gioberti, Lampedusa, reveal to one the difference. Trevelyan loved simple Sicilian folk as much as those of the mainland. He seemed to have overlooked the fact that Sicilians invented the Mafia.

*

In the hoary old dispute whether history was a science or an art, Trevelyan took an irrefutable common-sense line. Two heads of the Cambridge School, Seeley and Bury, insisted that history was a 'science, neither more, nor less'. This was silly. He made the obvious distinction between collecting the *facts*, where one must be scientifically rigorous, i.e. always accepting the dominance of the facts, never altering them but adhering to the truth – as against their interpretation and what they signify.

Trevelyan accepted that some bias would enter in, sometimes even with a salutary consequence. He instanced Gibbon's obvious bias against Christian beliefs, which called forth in return a more just appreciation of the record. That however did not incline him to favour controversy: 'I should be inclined to say that of all such books – more or less one-sided books of controversy – that they are not more effective controversially because of their one-sidedness.' Even here he qualified. *'Ira facit versus,* and sometimes wrath writes history. But wrath is not a good thing in itself, though sometimes it cannot be detached from good work.'

This led him, in my view, to take too favourable a view of Carlyle. He defended him to me by making a sharp distinction between his early work, which he found sympathetic, and the later, which all must find repellent. Here one observes the extaordinary Victorian unawareness. Ten volumes on Frederick the Great, and never once did Carlyle perceive that Frederick was a pure homosexual.

I don't suppose that such inflexions surfaced in Trevelyan's mind either – there was little that was ambiguous or ambivalent with him. He did not go in for the small change of opinions about other historians, but surprised me once by his admiration for Lecky, whom I had not read. Otherwise I might have recognised it as a pointer, for Lecky was an independent, not a professional academic, a rationalist, a sceptical Liberal who went over to Unionism, becoming more conservative with age and experience of politics. Trevelyan thought Acton over-estimated, but appreciated his own successor, the Catholic monk, David Knowles, who wrote like an angel. Trevelyan wrote that he owed most to Firth, who lent him rare tracts and pamphlets on the

Stuart period. His admirable textbook, *England under the Stuarts*, was depreciated, in the *English Historical Review*, by a reviewer who never got round to writing a book himself – one of those. Trevelyan took no umbrage: the Olympian never noticed such people.

He expressed admiration for Sorel's classic *L'Europe et la Révolution française*. (I have read only the first volume, would that I had read all six!) He exposed the evil of the Jacobin Terror, 'which destroyed the brightest hope of the Revolution, and was unnecessary for its defence.' He thought poorly of the *émigrés* – what an irresponsible lot the French aristocracy were, who brought their fate upon themselves! The true heroes of the epoch to Sorel were the starved and ill-shod soldiers of the first Revolutionary armies. The tragedy was the misuse of their patriotism 'to revive the policies of Louis XIV in Republican dress, and to rob and torture Europe for twenty years. You will look in vain for such Olympian impartiality in Treitschke and Mommsen.'

Chapters of the *History of England* were given as Ford Lectures at Oxford. When the book came out it was a runaway success. It was a textbook, and yet more. There were the expected qualities, the vividness, the landscapes, precision, the common-sense and political understanding. In particular I admired the construction, the firmness and conciseness with which such a mass of material was brought under control, every chapter in proportion, each paragraph concise and firm.

The success of this book enabled him to take up residence at Hallington, a family house a few miles only from famous Wallington, of his boyhood and youth. He dearly loved Hallington (Holy-dene), which he recreated for the summers, where I regularly stayed with him.

He was a generous man, and bought Housesteads, the finest fortress on the Roman Wall, to present to the National Trust. Also a farm to go with it. Here he did some archaeological digging on his own, and brought up a tile which showed the presence of the very *ala* (wing) of the legion, which Kipling had imagined there in a story about the Romans in Britain. Trevelyan wrote to tell Kipling about this odd coincidence, a chance confirmation. I was the less surprised because I regarded Kipling as a Celt, with his abnormal gifts of intuition and second-sight.

Housesteads was just over the horizon from the garden where we sat out and talked, almost always history. Along the ridge had taken place some battle – was it Heavenfield? – in which the Teutonic incomers had beaten the native Celts. I found this unpleasing. Trevelyan, for all his inveterate Celtic name,* was an unreconstructed Anglian (though what strain came in with his mother's family, the Phillipses of Manchester?).

During his time as head of the History School at Cambridge he wrote his biggest book, *England under Queen Anne*, 'my best work, except perhaps for the *Garibaldis*'. It is odd that he should make that exception, for *England under Queen Anne* is a grand work. It was perhaps fated, certainly indicated, that he should finish Macaulay's job. This crossed his mind when a young man, and his books rolled out with a certain inevitability, in sequence hardly thought of – as mine have done. As if waiting there in the wings ...

He was attracted by 'the dramatic unity and separateness of the period from 1702–1714, lying between the Stuart and Hanoverian eras with a special ethos of its own'. Here was the literary artist's perception: it is evident that he was ever the artist. 'Then too I always liked military history, and the Marlborough wars are one of its greatest themes.' He twice visited the battlefield of Blenheim, noting how little it had changed since Marlborough's day. We may note that those games with scores of lead soldiers (of German manufacture) which had fascinated him at home, right up to the age of twenty, served a purpose.

As an appendix to the splendid panorama of his *England under Queen Anne* he published a small volume, *The English Revolution of 1688*. This he dismisses as 'a final clearance of my

---

* The name, properly pronounced Trevillian, and sensibly spelt thus in America, is Cornish for the homestead of Milyan, with regular initial mutation. The ancient manor-house, in the parish of St Veep near Fowey, now owned by my friend Raleigh Trevelyan, goes back some 600 years.

studies in that region of history'. In fact it is a final summing up of that great issue, which dominated political thought for the next century. After that little masterpiece we need no more on the subject. It puts paid to the silliness of James II's reign. Trevelyan has no Whig favouritism for the men who made the Revolution. There was nothing 'glorious' about it, except that it was carried through by the governing class without any loss of life. James II's great service was to have united the whole country against himself. Trevelyan was kinder about him than he deserved.

For the next three years he devoted himself to the life of Sir Edward Grey. The safety of this country largely rested in the care of this man, as Foreign Secretary in the years running up to 1914, those of the Naval Rivalry started by Germany, already the strongest military power on the Continent. As if that was not enough!

Trevelyan knew his Northumberland neighbour well. 'In his grand simplicity, he was the finest human being I ever came across.' In his private life Grey suffered an extraordinary sequence of disasters with patient fortitude. This also characterised his tenure of office, in which he was constantly under attack from Left-wing illusionists about the facts in Europe, the growing danger from Germany looking to *'Der Tag'*. The Kaiser had the hardihood to reproach the English government for a Foreign Secretary who was a mere 'country gentleman'. Himself had as Imperial Chancellor the brilliant, but treacherous, Prince Bülow, who betrayed him. Grey said a wonderfully simple thing: 'I have usually found that to do the right thing is the right thing to do.' I doubt if that English idiom could be translated into any European language.

Trevelyan's judgement was that 'in appalling circumstances, Grey had proved a very great Foreign Minister.' The record proves it. In 1914–18 Britain had for Allies a firm France, Russia, Italy, eventually the USA. In 1940, after twenty years of Tory ascendancy, Britain faced a Germany, in control of Western Europe, but alone.

Trevelyan intended to complement his History of England with a Social History. In circumstances of the Second War, when he was Master of Trinity, it proved impossible for him to do the research necessary for the earliest period. So he decided to treat the last *Six Centuries*, beginning with Chaucer's England. This made a good starting point. 'For in Chaucer's time the English people first clearly appear as a racial and cultural unit. The upper class is no longer French, nor the peasant class Anglo-Saxon: all are English.' Here was his undying inspiration – in spite of his name, Trevelyan was nothing of a Celt.

He didn't waste time on defending his treatment, or on defining his subject. He thought that the study of economic history was the chief new development, new territory for exploration, in his time. Nothing of that in the great historians of the past, though Macaulay had given a foretaste of social history, conscious of providing something new, in his famous Third Chapter. He had learned from Walter Scott.

Trevelyan saw social history as welling up from economic factors, with political conditions more conspicuous on the surface. He was open-minded enough to think that we could do with less political history, as is conventional – there certainly is too much of it – while the English could do with a bit more cynicism in their view of things. As a Victorian, living into the tragic twentieth century, he was too old to provide it. But we can tell what he thought of it all from his tell-tale phrase, 'the fall of European civilisation'.

He was content to describe social history as history with the politics left out. This was rather heavily criticised at the time. What matter? The Master's last big effort had the greatest success of his many volumes. He told me that in its first year it made £42,000. Of this, with double tax plus double super-tax in both Britain and USA, he paid out £39,000! 'What a waste!' I said, 'Why didn't you hand the book over to the National Trust?' He replied that he would have done if he had thought of it.

He retained something of his inherited Radicalism to the end. He said to me, 'I pay my taxes gladly.' This was very far from being my sentiment. He had mellowed from that bleak Rationalist creed as he grew older and was very sympathetic to his successor, Dom David Knowles, a Catholic medievalist (who wrote like an angel, like Powicke). I was surprised by his expressing marked favour for Lecky (he had no liking for Seely, and was right about Acton). Only now do I see why Lecky – two disillusioned Liberals, or perhaps rather Whigs.

For all our differences of inflexion, opinions, tastes – and the utter contrast in our backgrounds – I never had any doubt of his greatness as a man or his genius as an historian, and I was proud to have the confidence of such a man.

CHAPTER 2

Sir Charles Firth

Seventeenth-century England was Firth's chosen field, and no one knew more about it – certainly not Macaulay, nor even the voluminous S.R. Gardiner, whose work Firth greatly assisted for years. The chief early influence in maturing Firth was the large-minded Stubbs. But Gardiner's concentration on the seventeenth century settled Firth into it; while he was contributing over two hundred lives to the *Dictionary of National Biography*, authoritative and sufficiently complete. All Souls had helped Gardiner's research work, as the college had equally supported Acton's; and Firth succeeded Gardiner there as Research Fellow.

A perceptive comment on Firth was to the effect that he suffered three disadvantages: 'bad health, a private income, and a special subject'. He became a rich man, from the famous firm of steel manufacturers at Sheffield (also at Pittsburgh in the USA). This enabled him – besides many private charities – to build up a magnificent library at his house in North Oxford, filled with rare books and Civil War tracts, pamphlets, first editions of texts, literary and historical.

When G.M. Trevelyan came over to consult some rarity, Firth said to him quizzically, 'You interested in writing about these old fellows?' 'Yes, aren't you?' 'No,' said Firth, 'only reading them.' This was like his somewhat wry humour, unfair to himself. For, in fact, he wrote a considerable amount, and edited still more. When I consider it all I find it very impressive, and I greatly admire its quality, the high standards it sets, the accuracy and good judgement, the impartiality and fairness. It offers a contrast to the bias and partiality of so much of recent writing on the period – pro-Parliament, pro-Puritan, pro-Levellers and Diggers, even holding up lunatic sects, Ranters, Soul-sleepers, Fifth Monarchy men, to admiration. None of that nonsense in the solid Yorkshireman that Firth was. Not that he had any illusions about the other side either. He was an impersonal historian; yet he appreciated the personal, the biographical in history – touches of his own personality come through and make his writing live.

He had been interested in Oliver Cromwell since schooldays, through Carlyle's rhetorical book. Firth's own biography of the great man, more judicious and utterly reliable, was his first book to alert the public to the fact that here was a master.

What are the qualities that stand out in his work, and help us to define it?

Altogether he did a mass of editing text and sources, along with his own books. We might call him a 'sources man', always keen to elucidate and correct sources upon which the historical account rests. To this end his special collections. He was exceptionally widely read in early English literature, and co-operated notably with Walter Raleigh in bringing into being the Oxford School in that subject. He also helped largely to create our School of Modern Languages. This interest in literature inspired a number of distinguished essays and specialist articles. Further, it underpinned the history, gave it more resonance.

Surprising, for a man who was so little of an aesthete, was his exceptional knowledge of portraits, prints, engravings, depictions of persons of the past: his interest was historical, in their characters. It was this that enabled him to produce a splendid illustrated edition of Macaulay's History, with a critical commentary.

Again, though Firth was wealthy, his inflexion was far from élitist, it might almost be said to be populist. In a concise survey of 'Ballads and Broadsides' – of which he had a rich collection – he wrote, 'These remnants of the popular literature of the time show how the people lived, and what they thought, the stories with which they were familiar, and the allusions which they could understand.' Not that his interest was restricted to the least interesting stratum of society, of which we have too much from academics today. Interesting people are more interesting than uninteresting ones.

'Shakespeare was as familiar with the English ballads of his time as Burns was with the songs of Scotland. ... The ballads which Shakespeare quotes are always those which were most popular and best known.' They supply evidence on the character of his audience, but also on his own tastes and way of work. He picked up the latest ballads cried in the streets as well as earlier ones printed as broadsides, just as – with his acute 'box-office' sense – he caught up current events and concerns into his plays. 'Often the same event attracted both the ballad-maker and the dramatist,' Firth pin-points, 'When the classics had been thoroughly ransacked, or classical stories had ceased to attract, English history supplied fresh materials.'

This brief remark concisely sums up the transition from early Elizabethan to later. Firth's literary essays show how much the historian has to contribute to the study of literature. It also shows up the impoverishment of a purely literary approach to the wealth of contemporary life in Shakespeare's plays. Pure ignorance to refuse to recognise it, though it needs the aid of the historian to interpret it.

For all the liveliness and variety of Firth's writings his main interest was always in research. When he became head of the History School as Regius Professor at Oxford, his inaugural lecture occasioned a resounding rumpus. In his downright Yorkshire way he uttered a challenge to the overwhelming concern of tutors with teaching and producing rounded products for government service and their place in society. He did not enter a tactful plea for more research so much as demanded it.

College tutors drew together to sign a joint protest, and a controversy ensued. The upshot was unfortunate, for the embattled tutors sent the university's most eminent historian into a kind of 'Coventry'. They didn't send people to his lectures, they isolated him. My own tutor, Feiling at Christ Church, once mentioned Firth's seminar; when I ventured to go only three or four people were present, and of course an undergraduate was out of place. Nevertheless, a year or two later, when I proposed to research into what precisely had been the consequences of the Reformation in my own native county, it was over dinner at All Souls that he at once suggested the crisp title, 'Tudor Cornwall'.

He was a formidable man, not easy of approach – Powicke thought him 'severe', though austere would be a better word. (He had a sad home-life.) By nature he was reticent, but underneath the reserve was a reservoir of kindness, sometimes lit up by a wintry smile. He was capable of a tease. As a young Fellow, I had a crush on Newman and collected his first editions. The drawing of him in Oriel Senior Common Room I thought 'beautiful'. 'But a silly face,' said the old boy. Come to think of it in my own old age, I think he was right. Newman's credulity was bottomless – fancy being willing to credit the flotation of the Holy House of Loreto from the Holy Land! Fancy crediting the liquefaction of the blood of St Januarius at Naples!

Newman was fundamentally feminine (hence the fuss he made over his own chastity – no problem: he was homo-erotic, in love with Hurrell Froude). Firth was heavily built, entirely masculine; but with shapely head and pointed beard, he had a rather Continental look, like a distinguished French *savant*. Paradoxical again, for, a sedentary man (slightly lame), he rarely travelled on the Continent and was entirely English in his interests. Actually Firth went back to the great Bishop Stubbs, creator of the Oxford History School. A down-to-earth countryman, Stubbs said of examinees, serving up his own lecture stuff to him, 'Do they expect me to drink my own piss and eat my own dung?'

Oliver Cromwell, as the Grand Regicide, was a subject of reprobation, until Carlyle – who had a shrewd perception of character – took him up. Gardiner, as a direct descendant of the great man (and a Plymouth Brother!), was of course sympathetic. So was Firth, appreciative and understanding of the 'magnitude of his mind'. A marked quality of his biography is the judicious use of quotations – Oliver speaking for himself, revealing himself as not the hypocrite people thought him, for

15

his sudden changes as circumstances demanded. A practical pragmatist, he *was* a masterly politician.

It was not to be expected that Firth, with his reticence, would go in for any psychological probing. He tells us that Oliver had a vehement temper, and was subject to depressions, but not that he was a manic-depressive, an hysteric, given to bouts of horseplay. They served a similar purpose of release from tension as Abraham Lincoln's off-colour jokes. Firth himself was Puritan in temperament, but had no religious belief. He realised well that Cromwell's primary concern was with 'God's people', the Puritans, i.e. he was a party man, and they were an 'armed minority'. 'So the rule of the Puritans, *founded with blood and iron*, fell without a blow.'

The Puritans were a small revolutionary minority (like Jacobins, or Bolsheviks), contrary to the vast majority of the nation and indeed the spirit of the English people at large. Firth does not go into the nonsense of their religious beliefs. They *all* thought, including Cromwell himself, that the succession of their victories in the field were 'God's providences', when they were only circumstances. 'Look at circumstances,' said Cromwell, 'they hang so together.' Well, what about 1660? Was that God's providence too? It knocked the bottom out of their argument, showed that their expectations were nonsense. Cromwell thought Catholics were beyond the pale of civilisation, as they thought he was – rather un-Christian sentiments on either side. Civilised persons, like Charles I and Laud, did not think in such terms.

The sceptical – and ultimately more English – mind of William Shakespeare observed, 'Men may construe things, after their fashion, clean from the purposes of the things themselves.' Firth did not point out that the Cromwells were Welsh by descent, though he noticed their kinship with the Williamses, the original family name.

Firth had a good understanding of character, not distorted by prejudice. One observes this in his thorough treatment of Macaulay. 'Macaulay had the mental habits of a politician, not those of a historian ... He naturally took a partisan attitude and scorned neutrality.' I'd have been a neuter in the Civil War, or gone abroad, like the sensible Hobbes. Macaulay 'was not troubled by intellectual doubts' – one recalls Melbourne wishing that he were so certain about anything 'as Tom Macaulay is about everything'. No doubt this gives firmness of line to Macaulay's History, as against the more variable, less assured, Froude. Still, it is interesting that Firth thought Macaulay the superior. (Oxford underestimated Froude, Cambridge overestimated Macaulay.)

Firth did not overestimate Cromwell; he did not think him so great a man as Caesar or Napoleon, if only because he operated on a smaller scale. He gives us a judicious estimate of William III, all the more of an heroic figure because perpetually dogged by ill health. The portrait of his Queen Mary, torn between father and husband, is so sympathetic as to be almost gallant. Nor does he elaborate on James II's religious foolery, for which he threw three kingdoms away and caused endless trouble to everybody. (Why shouldn't one recognise it? Formerly conventional politeness, or flummery, held historians up from speaking out.)

I like best Firth's Essays, where he speaks out more himself. Though his own views on history were impersonal, he well understood the importance of the biographical – all the more revealing. 'The *Pilgrim's Progress* is so closely related to the life of Bunyan that it is impossible to appreciate the one without some knowledge of the other … Bunyan's allegory is the generalisation of his own experiences, shadowing the incidents of his own history. He put the essence of his own life into the story; put into it reproductions of the life he saw round him, and recollections of the books he had read, made his actors real men and women.' What Firth tells us is all we need to know about John Bunyan, simplicity itself. It is a much subtler and more complex matter to understand how the experience and work of William Shakespeare affect each other.

No one has revealed, as Firth did, how much of Swift's own experience and political background are there in *Gulliver's Travels*. We easily recognise Sir Robert Walpole and his party set-up under George I in the first two books. But few of us realise how much of Irish Affairs and Anglo-Irish relations went into Books III and IV.

Firth liked the plain homespun of Burnet's style as against the 'elegant verbiage' of Bishop Sprat. That disapproving phrase speaks for Firth all through. Burnet first learned to appreciate and describe character by writing biography. Then, graduating to history, Burnet thought that 'of all men those who have been themselves engaged in affairs are the fittest to write history, as knowing best how matters were designed and carried on.'

Firth was above all interested in the history of action, with an unexpected keenness for naval and military affairs. He wrote a standard work on *Cromwell's Army*, and left two volumes, curiously enough, of Regimental Histories, for Godfrey Davies to polish up and finish. Another standard work was on *The House of Lords during the Civil War*. These special studies distracted him from the big work of finishing the Interregnum, following upon Cromwell's death in 1658, up to the reversal of the Puritan *épopée* in 1660. That too was left to Davies, Firth's assistant and devoted follower.

Homer occasionally nods. It is somehow consoling that the most unimpeachable of historians could miss a point. When Firth edited the Memoirs of Edmund Ludlow the Regicide, he failed to notice that the original text had been bowdlerised and smoothed over by John Toland, its editor, to suit the taste of the more rational audience of the eighteenth century. Ludlow's true text had been full of his Fifth Monarchy delusions and prophecies, ranting lunacies.*

Because of the tutors' feud with their professor, Firth could never get a job for the excellent Davies in Oxford. He was forced to take refuge in the Huntington Library, where he devoted himself to research (as I did later). There could be no happier

---

* See Edmund Ludlow, *A Voyage from the Watch Tower*, ed. A.B. Worden. We should be grateful for a biography of Toland, an original and fascinating figure. 'It is a mark of Firth's stature that his edition of the *Memoirs* will nevertheless remain of immeasurable value.' (p.vii.)

place for work, with its rich library and magnificent collections, equally devoted to history and literature.

There he finished up Firth's work for him, and produced *The Earlier Stuarts* volume in Clark's Oxford History of England. A work conscientious and reliable, following in the master's footsteps, impersonal, uninspired.

His wife also was a dedicated researcher, weevilling away at some uninspiring subject – I cannot remember what: something administrative. She was the daughter of an unmemorable, if magisterial, professor of economic history, Edwin F. Gay. She did not hold with my more personal view of history. Oh, dear no! Her father had brought her up the way history should be written. She expressed extreme disapproval* of my *Ralegh and the Throckmortons*, based on research into the Throckmorton Diary in the Cathedral Library at Canterbury. I should have published it in its original form, *verbatim* and *in extenso*. This, without ever having seen it! She had no idea of it – three folio volumes, hundreds of pages of minute detailed accounts. Unreproducible, let alone publishable. The best one could do with it was to skim the cream of its valuable new information about Ralegh, add it to his biography – it revealed much that was hitherto unknown, about his disgrace with the Queen, the birth of a son unknown to history, etc – and place it all in the perspective of the family background of Raleghs and Throckmortons. That is precisely what I did: I doubt if this prissy academic even read the work.

When her own book came out I was able to compliment her on a work of 'marmoreal perfection'. She took the point: it was of course totally dead, and unreadable.

* 'I could have killed you!', she said, somewhat to my surprise.

CHAPTER 3

Sir George Clark

G.N., as we called him, was an exceptionally accomplished historian. In personal conversation he was more amusing, alert and vivacious, bubbling with fun and jokes, full of ideas; he was extraordinary good company. Little of this came through in his work. For he came up under the rule of Firth, with his addiction to impersonality. When young, I made this reflection upon his admirable survey, *The Seventeenth Century*. He took it well from his junior, admitted that it was a defect and said amenably that he would reform.

He had good luck in the 1914–18 War, for he was early taken prisoner. By some arrangement he was transferred to Holland where he had relations. In confinement there he had plenty of time for reading, research, and languages; he became expert in Dutch and German, and told me that he had embarked on Russian. He was a markedly *clever* man. When he came back to Oxford he made good use of his expertise. His first book was *The Dutch Alliance and the War against French Trade* – the period of William III; and, since he lectured on Dutch history, as undergraduates we thought he was dull. How wrong we were!

His generalising book on his chosen field, the seventeenth century showed his comprehensive grasp, his wide knowledge, especially of the sources in several languages, and his openness to ideas. I forget what it was that I wished him to go on to – some comparable conspectus, I think. But he busied himself in all sorts of jobs, administrative and editorial – for some years he was editor of the *English Historical Review*, a prestigious but time-consuming job. He told me that his energy was such that he never tired. He was a busy, fussy little man, compact with energy. But this meant that he did not have the obsessive devotion to the task of a great historian like G.M. Trevelyan or Sam Morison in the USA.

Clark next took on the big job of editing a new Oxford History of England. This was well conceived, but must have taken up a lot of his time – his correspondence about it is illuminating. For it he wrote his own admirable textbook on the Later Stuarts. He told me that he fancied doing the final volume himself on the twentieth century, through much of which he had lived. In the event he handed it over to his former pupil, A.J.P. Taylor. Earlier Taylor had been venomous about his old tutor – but Clark was a timorous, tactful man, who had a rewarding way of feeding the hand that bit him. Consternated by this choice, I protested to G.N., who said agreeably, 'Well, he'll have me on top of him.' One curious circumstance was that both of them agreed in depreciating Churchill. This was not only prejudice on Clark's part but a relic of his early Leftism. Still, it was a defect: it showed lack of imagination and of appreciation of genius. Meanwhile he had changed gear to get out of tutoring and become Professor of Economic History at All Souls. Professor Clapham from Cambridge, doyen of the subject, railroaded Clark into the job, against Lipson who had been Reader in it for many years and expected to succeed to the chair. This was sad. I had proposed turning the Readership into a professorship at All Souls, and Clapham quoted my article on Clark's historical work (in the *Criterion*) in the election. Clark *said* that he was a monomaniac for the subject; he had something new to contribute and was able enough for anything.

Books eventuated, one of them good for a joke: *Guide to English Commercial Statistics, 1696–1782*. G.N. chortled, 'I have at last succeeded in writing a book that not only nobody will read, but nobody *can* read even if they try.' What was the point of that? – articles would have done well enough. He made an attractive transition with his *Science and Social Welfare in the Age of Newton*. This showed his perennial freshness of mind and openness to new ideas. It was exceptional for a regular historian to take up the history of science and to be capable of coping with it.

Always on the move, G.N. now made another move and became Regius Professor of Modern History at Cambridge in succession to Trevelyan. Odd as this seemed, there was something appropriate about it. I felt that Clark, with his interest in science and his flair for statistics, had a Cambridge inflexion of mind, while Trevelyan, with his romantic attitude to the past and his literary flair, was more in tune with Oxford. (Actually Trevelyan when young had tried for a scholarship at Oriel. Evidently some unimaginative don had failed there. It would have been exciting to have Trevelyan following in Froude's shoes – two men of genius.)

Clark did not remain long at Cambridge; he was shortly back at Oriel as Provost. He and Barbara were always chopping and changing their residence. When I first knew them they lived appropriately in Cromwell's House at Marston – one half of the manor-house Cromwell had occupied at the surrender of Oxford. There G.N. had edited the Chuchwardens' Accounts of the parish (he was an Anglican, a religious believer.) At another time, living in the Cotswolds, he wrote, as a parergon, a little book on the Campden Mystery, a piece of detection.

He did not remain long as Provost of Oriel, he found it a bore: administrative chores were not to his taste, though he undertook them – as President of the British Academy, for instance. It was in retirement, free of these chores, that he was able at last to give himself wholly to his *métier* as historian. He fulfilled his continued interest in science in his *magnum opus*, a two-volumed *History of the Royal College of Physicians*. A splendid job in which his double interest in the history of science and social welfare came together. He had indeed such vivacity of mind, such a spread of interests that he could not possibly fuse them all into a great work. In earlier years he was much interested in the history of war, and fancied making this a life-work. This was not to be – it was beyond him: concentration was not his forte, but diversity.

For a last work he brought together what, I suppose, had formed lectures as professor in a book on our history as a whole: *English History: a Survey*. It was a work worthy of remark, though it received little. It had none of the little thumbnail

22

portraits that enlivened Feiling's bigger History of England, nor
the sense of landscape that gives poetry to Trevelyan's History
(for history and poetry are not antithetical but go together).
Clark's book is, like himself, concise and concentrated.
Characteristic of it was that its whole approach was
governmental. He was interested in institutions, and the way
things were done. I was not, but I was all the more appreciative
of one who was and could enlighten one in this crepuscular field.

So I wrote a laudatory review in the *New York Times* and a
complimentary letter, which pleased the old boy now well on in
his eighties. He went straight into the kitchen to read it to
Barbara (very much his mentor), and wrote to me (it was Easter
time) that it had given him more pleasure than a papal blessing
from the balcony of St Peter's.

Difficult to sum him up, he dispersed himself in so many roles.
He suffered from cold feet – the family even charged him with it:
he was not the person to stick his neck out either for causes or
persons. He was good enough to ask me to become his colleague
as tutor at Oriel (he would have left me to do the work). But I
never wanted to be a tutorial hack, I was fixed on writing, and
writing history meant dedication to research. I do not think that
Clark was a dedicated man, he played too full a part in the life of
his time – all of it to the good.

When young he had been very much on the Left, a close
companion of G.D.H. Cole in his activities, partnering him in the
Oxford tram strike before 1914. No one knows now that G.N. put
in for the headship of Ruskin College, a Trade Union affair, at
Oxford. (That was a lucky escape.) The experience of the war
must have made a difference. G.N. changed gear, perhaps
convictions. He influenced my mind with a conclusive remark
when he said, in a moment of truth, 'It is the Intellectuals who
are the trouble with the Labour Party.' (C.R. Attlee: 'The
intelligentsia can always be relied on to take a wrong view of any
question.') This quiet remark, made at the outset of a
perambulation of Addison's Walk, influenced my mind for good.
I suddenly saw how right he was – the hopeless crew around
Kingsley Martin, editing the *New Statesman*; the weathercock
Dick Crossman; the whole *Tribune* group who, though on the

extreme Left, played Beaverbrook's game (paid by him) in attacking the responsible Labour leadership. Though an intellectual myself, I agreed with Attlee and Ernest Bevin about them.

G.N. became a man of government, a *bien pensant*. G.D.H. Cole thought ruefully that Barbara had a part in this. I dare say. But Douglas Cole never grew up – according to Attlee, 'the perpetual undergraduate'.

CHAPTER 4

Sir Keith Feiling

Keith Grahame Feiling, half-Scotch, was a nephew of the novelist, Anthony Hope, and a first cousin of Kenneth Grahame, author of *The Wind in the Willows*. So it was presumed that he would write. In fact he was not a good writer, but a better historian.

He was a dedicated tutor most of his life at Christ Church, Oxford. During his time the college had an exceptional run of Firsts in the History School. Never again. A Balliol man by origin, then a Fellow of All Souls, he did not much care for the Cathedral establishment at Christ Church, Dean and Canons occupying so much of the ecclesiastical desert of Tom Quad, and absorbing so much of the revenues. A tutorial type, he would have liked to reduce them. He might have said, with a young cleric hoping for preferment, 'Kilcanon Gate – would that it would function!'

Nevertheless his attitude, or inspiration, was romantic. He told David Cecil (he and I were his pupils) that every morning, when he came into college through Wolsey and Wren's Tom Gate, he felt a lift at heart. Practically his last book was *In Christ Church Hall*, an account of the serried portraits of famous men who had come up as undergraduates 'to make or mar'. There were all those Prime Ministers and bishops, John Wesley, John Ruskin, Lewis Carroll and, to me of special interest, Bishop Trelawny.

Feiling was a romantic Tory, rather than a plain Conservative, he thought of himself as a philosopher of Toryism, and wrote pamphlets about it – not much in that. A Balliol careerist, he had hoped for a political career; nothing came of it, anyway with his stammer he was not much of a speaker. Nor did he arrive at our Chichele Professorship until too late, for Sir Charles Oman, who had no retiring age and no pension, held on too long. Feiling would say, 'While there is death there is hope.'

His was an achievement worthy of respect – much above average dons – considering all his tutorial drudgery. He was known primarily as the historian of the Tory Party. His first fat book on its history, 1640–1714, from its origin in the Civil War to its downfall with the death of Queen Anne, came out in 1924, while I was an undergraduate. Though I had no money, I loyally bought it, and got rather bogged down in its details. Feiling's book had not the structure of one by Trevelyan, and his style was, like his speech, faltering.

Years later he produced *The Second Tory Party, 1714–1832*. I gave this a too-favourable review, for it had a fundamental fault. Feiling filled the story with the ins-and-outs at Westminster, where governments were all Whig right up to the end of the century. The Tories were in a perpetual minority – the ins-and-outs were all Whigs.

Richard Pares, our best authority on the eighteenth century, summarises: 'To talk of Whig and Tory, or of Party, as if these terms meant the same thing throughout the 18th century is to imply a fallacy which is now exploded. The Parties of 1760 were certainly not the same as those of 1714.' No doubt – but this may be missing something important. Horace Walpole wrote even more summarily: 'All the sensible Tories I ever knew were either Jacobites or became Whigs; those that remained Tories were fools.' Pares comments, 'And he spoke very truly.'*

My comment on these professionals here is a simple one: they were all thinking of Westminster, not the country at large.

The proper place to look for the continuity of Toryism was in the country, the localities. There in country parishes with the local squires and clergy, in towns and cities, cathedral closes – not with the bishops at Westminster – the Tory Party held on strongly, though only a small minority in Parliament. The cathedral city of Lichfield was where Dr Johnson got his

* Richard Pares, *George III and the Politicians*, 71–2.

Toryism. The Wesleys in the Lincolnshire countryside were a typical clerical Tory family. Oxford was Tory, with a sentimental Jacobite minority. And Namier tells us that the remote, rural North-West was a 'Tory belt'.

Feiling had no interest in *local* history; frustrated in his political hopes, he was glamourised by the boring party game at Westminster. Trevelyan wrote of him that he was 'more interested in religious, political and constitutional issues than in the social and economic'. I do not think that he was interested in religious issues, either – except that in his chosen seventeenth century religion was politics. It might be fair to say that Feiling, pathetically, was all politics. – Even his second work of research, *British Foreign Policy, 1660–72*. I do not remember this book, all petty detail again, for by this time I had been diverted into politics, and was struggling to write *Politics and the Younger Generation*. This was due partly to the dominant interest of All Souls in public affairs, partly to my being kept tutoring in political theory. Anyway I expect a good Tory like Feiling had some difficulty in explaining the divagatory policy of Charles II, eventually selling out to Louis XIV. Nor was Feiling a very clear-minded writer.

He was at this time engaged in contributing articles to *The Times* on more recent politicians, brought together in *Sketches in 19th Century Biography*.

Next he was asked by the family to write the official biography of Neville Chamberlain. I thought that the punishment fitted the crime, for he had been a supporter of this narrow-minded politician with no knowledge of Europe. I was amused to note that as a young man Chamberlain had been sent to the West Indies to grow sisal. It turned out that sisal wouldn't grow there, but Chamberlain went on trying and trying before he was forced to give up. This was to give him credit for persistence and determination. What about intelligence – when sisal wouldn't grow there? Just like his persistence with Appeasement.

Feiling's next biography, *Warren Hastings*, was more creditable. He had the advantage of knowing the background of that splendid career, for Feiling had spent his wartime service, during the First German War, in India. All the same, Penderel Moon's biography of Hastings for my Series was a more original performance, for he was able to portray the career from the Indian point of view. Hastings was exceptional in his concern with historic Indian culture, both Muslim and Hindu; he even pursued Sanskrit. I don't suppose Feiling felt any sympathy for the Whig miscreants, who made Hastings' life miserable for saving British rule in India, during the crises of the American and French Revolutions.

I remember a rather snide comment on Lady Chelmsford, not the most tactful of Vice-Reines, doing her round of officers in hospital. It was like Feiling's remark on our diminutive Dean, married to a large voracious man-eating American, to the effect that the Cat might eat up the Canary.

I preferred remarks that revealed his romantic feeling for the past. Out in the Cotswolds his wife had heard an old shepherd say, 'I shall be seventy, come Gunpowder day.' At home we always celebrated it as Guy Fawkes' day (the fool!), 5th November. It was like Oman's wife hearing an Oxford townswoman greeting her husband on leave from the Army, 'Marry come up, here's John.' Quite Shakespearean.

After the Second War Feiling at length succeeded to Oman's chair at All Souls, 1946–50. On his retirement I tried, when Sub-Warden, to get Feiling re-elected as Fellow, but was defeated as usual by my juniors. More regrettably, he was never elected a Fellow of the British Academy, though he had done far more research and contributed more than many among them. Why this neglect? I suspected Namier of obstructing, but G.N. Clark should have seen justice done.

During all these later years Feiling was at work on his finest book, his History of England. This final effort showed him at his best, earlier faults remedied. The structure was firm and, for all the ground covered, he did not get lost in detail. He had one gift which neither Trevelyan nor Clark possessed – that of depicting his characters in living thumbnail sketches.

*

4. Sir Keith Feiling

At Christ Church the teaching was shared by two more historians. I never felt that J.C. Masterman was really interested in the subject. He was more of a schoolmaster, who saw to it that we did our weekly essays, and that got us forward.

E.F. Jacob was deeply interested in the Middle Ages, though he couldn't put it across. He left to become professor at Manchester, a regular colony of the Oxford School, and then back to All Souls as Chichele Professor. He began with Powicke's thirteenth century, then moved out to the fifteenth and the Conciliar Movement. I got him to write the biography of Henry V in my Series. Very churchy, he had that qualification for a medievalist and supervised the editing of Archbishop Chichele's immense Canterbury Register in four volumes. He had a good command of languages, but an extraordinary facility for making minor errors – I could not understand it. Clark recruited him to write the Fifteenth Century volume in the Oxford History. I read it with appreciation, thinking that McFarlane could have done a firmer, if more secular, job. But, then, he would never have produced it at all.

CHAPTER 5

Sir Arthur Bryant

How good a historian was Arthur Bryant? By the academic world he was disconsidered and overlooked; by English society, particularly in London, he was thought to be the greatest of living historians. Both opinions were wrong. But it is difficult to strike a balance and give a just estimate of his work. He was the most popular historian of his time – and above all an emotional, even a sentimental, one.

His work emerged from a prodigious mass of journalism and topical booklets to catch the moment. I once heard him say, at Boughton, that as a schoolboy he had had to write an essay every week, and he had been doing it ever since. This was true: he was scribbling all the time, in London, in country houses, in trains, on board ship, even in taxis.

Yet in this mountain heap there was much good stuff. He was always alive and had a good sense of humour, a wonderful feeling for landscape and country life. He wrote endearingly about cats and dogs. He had a prodigious memory for verse, if a conventional taste: he did not go so far as to appreciate T.S. Eliot, or post-Eliot poetry.

Some of these qualities come through in his serious work, with which only we are concerned. His charm comes through in his writing, a man of exceptional gifts. He did not shine at Harrow or Oxford (Queen's College), though his wartime service in the then RFC (now RAF) and in France served as some apprenticeship for a military historian.

He came to history in an oddly direct way all his own. He had shown no aptitude or interest at school or university, when he suddenly discovered the delights of research and fell in love with it. It happened, like a conversation, one winter at an old country house, Somerford in Cheshire, where he penetrated into the archives of the Shakerleys.

There he worked away under the portrait of old Peter Shakerley, 'dearest of all the dead men and women I grew to care for. Though the house he built is now perished and the tall trees he planted all felled, his careful, far-seeing spirit still broods over the wasted parklands of Somerford, and in the little panelled chapel which alone survives of the ordered paradise he created in what was formerly a wilderness – and has now, by man's folly and greed, been made a wilderness again.'

There was Bryant's inspiration. His best qualities were his passion for the English past, and his gift for giving expression to it, calling back above all its *life*. As for research, he never gave up on it, and did more – in spite of his variegated active concerns, markedly in education – than those who overlooked him.

He began his historian's career with a fine flourish, in the dismal year of 1931. His biography of Charles II appealed to the public at once and became a best-seller. For all the attractiveness of the portrayal this academic was not persuaded. Everything was described in Charles II's favour, not a word of criticism. But hadn't he jeopardised, if not betrayed, the country's interests by falling in with Louis XIV? True, the Whigs accepted bribes from him too. But the duplicity of the party game furthered Louis' march to ascendancy in Europe, which it took twenty years of European warfare later to reduce.

Next year Bryant followed with a little book on Macaulay which, appealingly, was based on original research among his papers at Trinity College, Cambridge. All the while Bryant was engaged on heavy research into the voluminous records, papers and manuscripts of Samuel Pepys. The first volume of this massive biography, *The Man in the Making*, appeared in 1934. This substantial volume was followed, in Bryant's manner – making the most of things – by a neat little book, *The England of Charles II*, and then an edition of the King's Letters and Speeches.

31

It happened that I read Bryant's Pepys book in hospital in a low state after a couple of operations. The book's sparkling vivacity, the naughty goings-on at the Restoration Court, the fun and frolics, the sense of *life*, helped me back to life. I have never owed so much to a book; grateful, I wrote the author a fan-letter, first I had ever written.

This was the beginning of a long friendship. Arthur asked me over to his little Elizabethan house at Claydon, and introduced me into the famous house of the Verneys, with whose published Letters I was familiar. He of course knew the originals and the family.

Among his multifarious activities, lecturing (he was a most winning lecturer) – he lectured across country for the Workers' Educational Association as well as at the Conservative college at Ashridge, and running an Arts and Crafts School at Cambridge – he plodded on at Pepys. He *was* a plodder, and in 1935 produced his second big volume, *The Years of Peril*. Bryant was entirely on Pepys's side in the partisan charges against his administrative record. Here he was entirely justified: the little diarist was one of the finest servants the Royal Navy ever had. Even James II was a conscientious naval administrator.

This was followed by an enchanting anthology, *Postman's Horn* – inspired by Arthur's exquisite feeling for the past, and rendered still more valuable for the pieces that came from unpublished manuscripts. The third volume of Pepys, *The Saviour of the Navy*, came in 1938. Bryant varied his serious work by short popular books, like his sycophantic tribute to Stanley Baldwin, whom he admired. He recommended him to me as a master of committees. As a Labour candidate I recognised him (as did Churchill) for a masterly party manoeuvrer, who kept the Tory party in a big majority all through that disastrous decade.

In 1940 – of all years! – came a bombshell from Bryant, his book *Unfinished Victory*. Throughout the 1930s he was a supporter of the Tory Party's Appeasement of Hitler. To what a degree I did not realise, though we had a raging row on the subject, in a car all the way through his native Dorset.

I was thunder-struck when he charged Churchill – of all

people! – for the low state of our armaments and our unpreparedness for Hitler's War. This he charged to the Ten-Year Rule imposed in 1924, for reviewing defence needs. In the interval there was no need for rearmament. When Hitler came to power in 1933 there *was* – as anybody who read *Mein Kampf* and watched Germany at work should have known. The American ambassador wrote that all Germany was an armed camp.

I argued that the considerations of Policy came first, the requisite implementing it for defence came second. He couldn't see it. I repeated: First think out the right Policy, *then* implement it according to its needs and requirements. He went on and on obstinately repeating, 'the Ten-year Rule', and blaming Churchill. He couldn't see the intellectual point at stake. It showed up, what one knew all along, that, for all his first-rate gifts, he was intellectually second-rate. He was not a thinker.

The book came to Macmillan's. Harold Macmillan of course totally disagreed with it. The argument of the book was that we should go on making concession after concession, meeting Hitler's 'grievances', i.e. handing him his triumphs on a plate. This had already served to build up his rule in Germany, built up such a position that, if continued, we should be at his mercy. Couldn't Bryant see that? No – second-rate thinking. The Foreign Office saw it, and so did Churchill.

Harold Macmillan published the book: liberal-minded to a fault, he said, 'We are publishers, not policemen.' But they did not publish another book by Bryant, and he speedily did his best to climb back on the band-wagon. He never mentioned the book to me, and only once, in later years, remarked casually that he had been wrong. Even so, I never learned, until after his death, that he had gone farther: he had actually gone to Germany to reassure Hitler's adjutant of Britain's pacific intentions. Hitler could go ahead!

To such lengths were Appeasers prepared to go. He never dared to mention that enterprise to me – if I had known, it would have ended our friendship.

*

There was no question of Bryant's patriotism – his failing was muddle-headedness. He had plenty to keep him company – the vast majority of the House of Commons which supported Appeasement right up to the edge of the precipice. I called it 'the Unspeakable Assembly', adapting an historic phrase, *'la Chambre introuvable'*. In the very same year as *Unfinished Victory* he published his popular *English Saga*, to rehabilitate himself. Baldwin thought he had 'overdone' it.

During the following years he devoted himself to a fine trilogy, to keep our spirits up. This covered the long struggle with the French Revolution and Napoleon, and the eventual triumph of the Peninsular War. In 1942 came *The Years of Endurance* – such as we were going through at the time. Then, in 1944, followed *The Years of Victory* (good timing).

I found this volume exhilarating; it displayed Arthur's qualities at their best. He had a splendid eye for landscape and the topography of Spain, and was a good hand at the battle scenes, Talavera, Albuera, Badajoz, all the way to Pamplona and Vittoria, over the frontier and into France. All so vivid, I remember touches of it still. There was the Duke, always a sympathetic character, with an old Spanish country woman bringing him a bad egg for his breakfast. The Duke, with grave courtesy, ate it up. (One just couldn't!)

The war in the Peninsula went on so long that some of the officers brought over their pack of hounds – those were aristocratic days – and had fine runs, in the intervals of fighting, across that tawny, lion-coloured land.

In the last volume, *The Age of Elegance*, Arthur was equally at home. This covered the Regency years and after, Carlton House, and the Brighton Pavilion; the designing of the West End of London, Nash's Terraces, Regent's Park – to make the capital worthy of the victors of Waterloo. He was a man of taste, well equipped for all this. He loved beautiful objects and collected them, historic portraits, furniture, rugs, Aubusson carpets, snuff-boxes, *étuis*, Canton enamels. (Here I was willing to learn from him.)

There went along with this aristocratic taste – nothing modern however – a grand feeling for popular life and sport.

5. Sir Arthur Bryant

Regency life was a good deal of a rough-house; frequent mobs, riots in the streets – grandees had to run the gauntlet, but they were tough too. It was the age of pugilism and fisticuffs, the championship wrestling match of Polkinghorne and Abraham Cann.

Arthur's sympathies were all with the people, to a surprising extent. He was a true Tory, not confined by any party programme, open to some Radical ideas. He liked prize-fighters, old-fashoned Trade Unionists, and of course Army and Navy men, among whom he had a devoted following. His book was full of enjoyment – he was no Puritan – a tonic after the glum days of the war.

He was miles away from Bloomsbury intellectuals, at the opposite pole to Lytton Strachey in several respects – he was a devotee of what he regarded, with Louis XV, as *le beau sexe*.

Bryant had been brought up at Court, where his father was Comptroller of the Household to King George V. The paternal advice to his growing-up son was, 'Never trust a man who uses scent, my boy.' I suppose this referred to the excellent Lord Esher, Governor of Windsor Castle. The advice was quite unnecessary so far as Arthur was concerned.

The King had been badly educated by Hugh Dalton's father, a naval chaplain. As king, George V conscientiously did his best to correct this, steadily going through a reading list every year. When one of Arthur's books came out the poor old boy reflected sadly, 'See what *his* son has done!'

Parodoxically, though Bryant *was* more than a little sycophantic towards Prime Ministers Baldwin and Chamberlain, it is fair to say that he was not at all a snob – rather odd, and creditable in his circumstances.

Curiously enough, he maintained good relations with other historians: he was on friendly terms with Trevelyan and Neale, and my pupil, Veronica Wedgwood. He was a clubbable man, with seductive charm and some endearing eccentricities. As to publishing, he was very professional, quick on the mark. He extended his arm, from the large trilogy, to popular biographies of Nelson and Wellington.

*

Bryant was so much in the public eye, regarded by the uninstructed authorities as our foremost historian, the recipient of several 'honours' from them, that he was given some special commissions, such as to edit the Diaries of Alanbrooke, our best military brain. And again the record of the Green Jackets. (Even I was asked to write the official History of the RAF during the war, and the record of our DCLI – Duke of Cornwall's Light Infantry. I was quite incompetent for such jobs – only the Elizabethan age and Shakespeare for me!)

Bryant turned the bonus of the Alanbrooke material into two best-sellers of his own, *The Turn of the Tide* and *Triumph in the West*. I disclaim the competence to judge these works. He was engaged in a large, far-flung venture, yet another History of England in several volumes. Did we really need it from him?

He worked away at it conscientiously, calling on his friends for help. I was regularly made use of, as before, to criticise his text, though I found this rather a bore. He called in a young medievalist from Liverpool University to hold his hand over the Middle Ages. When he reached the volume of more concern to me, *The Elizabethan Deliverance*, I could not but recognise the freshness, the enthusiasm; also I was relieved to find that it was fundamentally sound. He followed the right authorities and stayed in the regular tracks.

However, I was not in sympathy with the last phase of his work. He went on and on playing the old gramophone record about the continuing glories of England. Really, in the Silly Sixties, the decline of the country, when it was all too evident that the great days were over – the end of the Empire, the hurried scuttle from Africa, the humiliation of Suez (the dreadful Foster Dulles, who had sabotaged us, said, 'Why didn't they go on with it?'), the crack-up of our position in the Middle East, the Americans taking over! How *could* he go on with the old record, when it was all over? I suppose it was popular.

How much of his work then remains – of all that mountain?

There was a good deal of honest research in it. It was not, as the irresponsible A.J.P. Taylor said, all 'scissors-and-paste'. Bryant stuck to his authorities and his frequent quotations represented genuine research. Thus his large work on Samuel

5.   Sir Arthur Bryant

Pepys certainly stands. His Regency trilogy offers an authentic picture of the age, vigorous and sympathetic – he was in tune with it, a qualification. I liked best his essays, collected in such books as *Historian's Holiday*. He was a *born* writer, as few are, and he dedicated himself, even obsessively, to his gifts, which were not those of a first-class intellect. His thinking was emotional, and that was of a piece with his gifts.

CHAPTER 6

H.A.L. Fisher

Of all the Oxford historians of my time H.A.L. Fisher was the most distinguished *writer* as such, a conscious practised artist. There was that strain in the family. There too his family belonged to the highest strain of Victorian art and letters, Julia Cameron, G.F. Watts, Burne-Jones, George Eliot, Tennyson – everybody. Thus he belonged to that intellectual cousinage – Leslie Stephens, Maitlands, Vaughan Williams, Darwins, Wedgwoods – depicted by Noel Annan as the *fine fleur* of their time. H.A.L. Fisher could not but be a very superior person. He was not an intimate man.

His father was the last Vice-Warden of the Stannaries, as he told me. Since tin-mining in Cornwall was declining to its end, the office was practically a sinecure. But it meant regular visits to Cornwall, where they enjoyed picnics, and walks over moors and cliffs, with Leslie Stephen and his daughters, Virginia and Vanessa, at St Ives – depicted in Virginia's *To the Lighthouse*.

Virginia Woolf has several references to her cousins, the Fishers, in her Diaries, always pinpricking and depreciatory. She describes them, improbably, as lacking in life. True, they were a bit lofty. But Virginia had a malicious streak: Trevelyan described her to me as a 'dreadful woman'. We must place on the other side of the account her struggle with two periods of madness, her courage and persistence in carrying through her work. *Her* sense of life was too tremulous and strained for balance and sanity.

Fisher was a man with a variety of gifts, set on giving expression to them all. Hence he spread himself too widely. He had an extraordinary capacity for work, along with speed in

38

accomplishing it. He did not waste much time in talk, communicating in conclusive sentences. A great writer concentrates on writing. Would Fisher have been a great historian if he had concentrated on his historical work? This is open to doubt.

His *Unfinished Autobiography* gives an enviable depiction of his boyhood at Winchester, undergraduate days at Oxford, and then his training for his task at the Ecole des Chartes in Paris in those good days. How lucky they were! He made the acquaintance of Renan. I detect the influence of Renan's *Souvenirs d'Enfance et de Jeunesse* upon his own memoirs; and more on his formation and general outlook. Renan was a conservative sceptic, intellectually liberal, Fisher was a liberal sceptic. Renan was a defeatist, as Celts are apt to be.

Fisher was very much at home in Paris; there was a French strain in his family and he spoke French fluently. Thus he could claim, 'I was the first to break with the established tradition that post-graduate study in historical science could only profitably be carried on among the Germans.' Later he noticed how deleterious the dominance of the German concept of universities had been in the newer academic institutions across the United States. Their own older institutions in the East were better, in accord with American traditions.

Fisher experienced a France full of grief and resentment at the Franco-Prussian War, and Bismarck's wrenching away of Alsace-Lorraine. If only the new imperial – and imperious – Germany could have contented herself with Alsace, where the population was more German (if not Germanophile), and left Lorraine to France – would it have made a difference? As it was, the young Englishman witnessed the Revanchist idiocies of Boulanger and Paul Déroulède.

However, when he got to Göttingen in due course he was in for a rude awakening. 'One day in the late autumn of 1890 a fellow member of the *Historische Verein* explained to me that Germany regarded Britain as her eternal enemy and predestined victim. We Britons had won an Empire by good fortune, when Germany was asleep, and we should lose it inevitably now that Germany was fully awake. Britain was Carthage, Germany was Rome.

Even if the first Punic War was not successful there would be other Punic wars to follow. [1914–18, followed by 1939–45?] Germany aspired to rule the world. Britain stood in her way. The stage was set for a great, an inexorable struggle.' The young German was able to inform the Englishman that 'Queen Victoria was a dipsomaniac. Why, if not in search of the national beverage, should she go to Scotland? And her eldest son a kleptomaniac.'

All this was new to Herbert Fisher. 'The idea of a European war in which our country was involved never entered our minds.' But this was Bismarck's Germany. 'The doctrine of the Punic Wars was abroad through Germany. Its fountain-head, so far as I could discover, was the deaf, violent Saxon Professor, Heinrich von Treitschke, who was then drawing large audiences to Berlin by his eloquent diatribes against Britain. This man held the leading chair in Germany, with its potent, radiating influence' – a position which the sane and civilised Swiss, the great Burckhardt, refused.

The English had no idea of these amenities in store for them, nor would they take telling when told of them in our time. They were of course continuous, and recognisable, with their popularisation and demotic vulgarisation in the creed of Hitler and Nazi Germany.

To return to the more congenial theme of historical study and what the young man learned in Paris. 'You must remember', Renan told him, 'that hysterical patients have a strong tendency to deceive.' He did not add that they also deceive themselves. From Taine young Fisher learned that physical causes had been neglected by historians and more attention should be paid to them. 'How often during the war of 1914–1918 was it not clear that statesmen, generals and admirals became suddenly less efficient through physical fatigue.'

It should be evident enough now that our leading men in the 1930s – MacDonald, Baldwin and Chamberlain – were not up to their job, worn out. Indeed Baldwin confessed to his old Harrow friend, Warden Pember at All Souls, that he was holding down a job which he was not physically capable of performing. It was even visible that MacDonald, half blind, was gaga. Neville Chamberlain must have had the cancer already from which he died shortly after leaving office. Why wouldn't they make way for younger men?*

Fisher learned from the eminent Fustel de Coulanges, whose *La Cité Antique* had struck a new vein and had prodigious influence at the time. 'Fustel had travelled on the high road which leads from the ancient to the modern world. It was exactly the route which I proposed to follow.' However, he did not regard the example and teaching of the Ecole des Chartes as supplying the most important part of historical training. 'The past cannot be reconstructed by men whose knowledge of life is solely derived from documents. His books will lack the perspective and the insight into reality which makes the past instructive to living men.' Fisher came to feel the need for practical experience. (At the same time of life I felt the need to fill myself out with the practical experience which I lacked. So perhaps my grinding apprenticeship in the Labour Party was not all loss.)

Taine even warned the young Fisher against excessive devotion to the Ecole des Chartes, as I came to see that one might get engulfed, buried in the catacombs, of the Public Record Office. Perhaps one might intuit the way Fisher would go. On the other hand, I detect a significance in a casual remark dropped about a companion of those days in Paris, Will Rothenstein: 'Perhaps if he had had less all-round facility he would have accomplished more as a painter.' Victorian menfolk were extraordinarily un-selfaware. Did it never occur to Fisher that this might apply to himself?

His first piece of writing was a tribute to Fustel, which Maitland published in the *English Historical Review*. And indeed with the ancient history of Greats behind him Fisher thought of continuing in that field. But France won. He revised Kitchin's textbook on French history. (As I translated and brought up to date Lucien Romier's *Histoire de France*, on voyages to and from America, across the States and into

---

* This was a theme of my *Politics and the Younger Generation*.

Canada. As an active politician Romier made French history *intelligible*.)

Then Fisher shifted gear to Germany, with a big book on *The Medieval Empire*, following in the tracks of the classic *Holy Roman Empire* of Bryce – the venerated ambassador in Washington, whose official biography Fisher was to write some years later. Next, a book that combined France and Germany in a more original way: *Napoleonic Statesmanship: Germany*. His intention was to follow this up in other countries. This he never did. He jumped into Tudor history, by contributing the volume on the early Tudors, 1485 to 1547, to Longman's History of England. I found this an attractive, congenial book – like all his writings; but it had not the firmness and mastery of Pollard's succeeding volume.

This was followed by a book on *Bonapartism*, and one of wider scope on *The Republican Tradition in Europe*. Fisher was a good European, with a Continental perspective. Meanwhile, he was teaching hard for New College in several fields, and made one of the editors of the admirable Home University Library. For this he produced the best short biography of Napoleon in any language, according to a French critic. He recruited the young Lytton Strachey to write for this his first book, *Landmarks in French Literture*. Fisher said to me, in his grand way, 'I gave Strachey his first chance.' Hitherto, Strachey had not been promising – but he was a connection, of course.

Maitland was a brother-in-law, and Fisher did a mass of work on him, after his early death – the greatest loss of all to our profession, for he was a man of genius. Fisher wrote a brief *Memoir*, collected his scintillating papers on unscintillating subjects, the history of law, in three volumes. This work was completed by editing Maitland's Lectures into a textbook on English Constitutional History, which we all used.

Thereupon Fisher had his initiation into public life, with his membership of a Royal Commission on the services in India, from 1912 onwards. This engaged his interest strongly; it took up the Anglo-Indian tradition of his family. He put a lot of work into it, the Report – which, it may be suspected, he had a large hand in writing – not appearing until 1917. By then he had moved fully into public life. In 1914 he accepted with alacrity the Vice-Chancellorship of the promising new University of Sheffield. This meant a relief from the heavy load upon a college tutor at Oxford in those days. R.W. Lee told me that he had taught forty hours a week. (As a Research Fellow of All Souls I was limited to twelve hours a week – more than any professor's stint today – besides examining and lecturing on political theory. I was never invited to lecture on sixteenth century history, my special period.) At Sheffield Fisher threw himself into the multifarious activities of wartime.

Suddenly, in December 1916, when Lloyd George formed his government to win the war, he called up Fisher to be Secretary of State for Education. It was an inspired choice on the part of that imaginative Prime Minister. Fisher entered politics in a very superior way, as a Cabinet Minister at the top – he had never been a mere M.P. any more than he had been a mere professor. For the next six years, as Minister of Education, he made history. It is no part of my scheme to tell that story, but he carried further the grand achievement of the Conservative Act of 1902 in creating a national system of secondary education. This was the work of a great civil servant, Sir Robert Morant, another Wykehamist, backed by Balfour, who gave constant support to Fisher's progressive plans, as did Lloyd George.

It is a tell-tale pointer that, in his autobiography, Fisher goes straight from his early days to his public career, omitting any consideration of his historical work. It is obvious which he considered the more important. He took to political life like a duck to water, and some of his comments have value and relevance today.

The generals of the 1914–18 War were a second-rate lot – with the possible exception of Allenby. Fisher, a positive reformer, was shocked that, from all the new armies raised since 1914, not a single general was promoted. They were all Regulars, left-overs from the antiquated Boer War – and frustrated Lloyd George to distraction. (Lord Salter told me that, walking with him in St James's Park, the Prime Minister wept at the tale of casualties from Passchendaele.)

Fisher also tells us that the Tories, who had thrown over the brilliant Balfour for the second-rate Bonar Law, were determined to throw over Lloyd George for creating the Irish Free State, ending the unworkable Union. They then opted for the second-rate Baldwin. How much the two men of genius, Lloyd George and Churchill, were missed in the Thirties, the apogee (and apotheosis) of Baldwin and Chamberlain!

Fisher fell with Lloyd George in 1922 and, as a Liberal, never saw office again. He remained on uselessly in Parliament for another four years, but writing, his biography of Bryce and a memoir of Vinogradoff. He gave a lead to a theme taken up by others with a notable lecture on *The Whig Historians*. There were other parerga, and he travelled. In French Canada he impressed audiences with his fluent French. In every field, political, historical, literary, he was an accomplished speaker. But what future was there for an out-of-work Liberal, ditched like so many others by the demise of the Party?

The Wardenship of New College fell conveniently vacant, and he was asked to stand for it. 'Yes,' he said, 'it may come to that.' This remark nearly cost him the job. He obviously regarded it as a *pis-aller*. '*Quelle chute!*' said Clemenceau, when the great pianist, Paderewski, became Prime Minister of Poland. Fisher missed the days when, as Cabinet Minister in the days of the Empire, telegrams from all over the world, with their information, arrived every morning on his desk. Oxford in its kindly way, told (or made up) a story. Fisher opened talk with a Rhodes Scholar with (a by no means improbable remark), 'When I was in the Cabinet with Mr Lloyd George' – still a world-famous name. The Rhodes scholar was supposed to have said, 'Come, come! Mr Fisher.'

He polished off his work as Warden in a couple of hours a day. He dutifully attended Chapel, appearing in his stall, somebody said, like an 'up-ended sarcophagus' having no part in the proceedings. A Renan-style Rationalist, he embarked on his grandest effort, a huge three-volumed *History of Europe*.

This Olympian survey combined his widespread reading in ancient, medieval and modern history – the lot. His Preface contained a statement of his credo. 'One intellectual excitement has, however, been denied me. Men wiser and more learned than I have discerned in history a plot, a rhythm, a predetermined pattern. I can see only one emergency following upon another as wave follows upon wave, only one great fact with respect to which, since it is unique, there can be no generalisations, only one safe rule for the historian: that he should recognise in the development of human destinies the play of the contingent and the unforeseen. This is not a doctrine of cynicism and despair. The fact of progress is written plain and large on the page of history; but progress is not a law of nature. The ground gained by one generation may be lost by the next.'

We of the last generation can appreciate that all too well today.

This statement of a disillusioned Liberal was much discussed at the time. It was natural that a practising politician should see one emergency following upon another. These are phenomena on the surface, many of them passing air bubbles occupying too much attention, taking too much space in the story. But what of the currents, the tides, the greater movements below the surface that carry us along, and most people are unaware of? It is the business of the historian to be aware of both, and, difficult as it is, to combine both in his writing.

This was my criticism of the book at the time. I dare say his practice was better than his creed. He said to me in the train to London, turning his classic features upon me, 'When I put down my pen I thought I should never take it up again.'

He took it up again to good purpose in *Our New Religion*, entirely in the spirit of Renan, in which he made fun of Christian Scientist credulity and the absurdities of Mrs Mary Baker Eddy. I still remember his joke on her theme that 'matter isn't real'. A well-heeled congregation totters out on the pavement of Park Lane – it might well have contained Lady Astor – with 'the ghost of an appetite in pursuit of a phantom of a lunch'. Philip Lothian was called on to review it in the Astor family paper, the *Observer*. Lothian was a convert (there was madness in the family): he sadly reproached the Warden of his college for his scorn, hoping that he would yet remain to pray. Some hopes! – like his hopes of Appeasing Hitler. He did a good job in the Washington Embassy, and died there without calling in a doctor. His friend, Lionel Curtis, uttered his epitaph: 'Philip died in the knowledge that he had been wrong.' What was the good of that? He should have *known* what Hitler and the Germans were up to – the reversal of the insufficient lesson of 1914–18.

Fisher himself was not anti-German. He said to me, at the time of our gravest danger from them, 'We must reckon on Germany always being a great power.' I found the thought, true enough, depressing.

The Second War drew Fisher once more, a man of seventy-five, into public service. In London he was knocked down by a lorry, from which accident he died. He was a devoted public servant, an eminent historian, and a good citizen of Europe.

CHAPTER 7

Sir Charles Oman

We of the first generation after the 1914–18 War under-estimated Oman, as his work is also overlooked today. A prime interest of his was military history, and in our innocence we thought that we had done with all that, and could ignore it. The holocaust of the First German War had more than decimated the governing classes of Britain and France, and we thought that that had been 'a war to end war'. We counted without the Germans, whose reactionary military elements did not recognise defeat and meant to reverse it. We thought that Oman was out of date, with his Right-wing views and his interest in war. It was we who were.

Secondly, born in 1860, he was before specialisation became acute and dominated the historical schools. As the *DNB* says of him, he was genealogist, archaeologist, numismatist. Brought up on Greats, he was based on ancient history, and began with a series of textbooks on Greece and Byzantium. His *Seven Roman Statesmen* was a good stand-by, and brought in regular returns for years.

From this he went on to early English history, and wrote a standard book on England before the Conquest. He next produced a work of original research on the great Peasants' Rising of 1381. All the while he was building up his knowledge of military history, techniques, castle-building, archery, the development of gunfire and similar amenities. This gradually took shape in two volumes, the Art of War in the Middle Ages and another on the Sixteenth Century. I read, or at least consulted, the second.

A delightful offshoot of all this was an illustrated book on

47

Castles, undertaken for the Great Western Railway. I appreciated that: it spoke to me, appealing especially to my West Country loyalty and love of architecture.

All the while, for thirty years, Oman was researching for his immense work, his History of the Peninsular War, in seven stout volumes. This in addition to his regular load of tutoring for New College, professoring, and being librarian of the Codrington. His lifetime of research would not have been possible but for his All Souls Fellowship: he regarded his election as the most fortunate thing that happened in his life. Many others have had reason to think so, without generously feeling it. Oman's college loyalty took amusing form. At his daughter, Carola's, confirmation the name Anima was conferred upon her (Collegium Omnium Animarum); and his son Charles was baptised Chichele, after our Founder, Archbishop Chichele.

A more important consequence was that, as librarian, he had the whole run of Vaughan papers in the Codrington at his disposal. Sir Charles Vaughan had been Britain's diplomatic agent in Spain during that war. Later, he was ambassador in Washington in the time of Andrew Jackson's Presidency. As a gallant bachelor, Vaughan could entertain Old Hickory's Egeria, Peggy Easton, whom the prudish ladies there would not receive. The President however said that she was as chaste as driven snow. Senator Sumner, who was not respectable himself, commented:

> Age cannot wither nor custom stale
> Her infinite *virginity*.

One doubts if a senator in these demotic days could make such a play on Shakespeare's words.

Napier's classic but controversial History of the Peninsular War is spoilt by party prejudice against the Tory government that conducted it. The war in Spain was the only way that Britain had of challenging Napoleon's military control of Europe. It was absolutely necessary to maintain the struggle against it. The younger Pitt was historically right to give Europe a lead – as he had been equally right in opposing the war against the American Colonies. Good judgement – the prime quality for leadership.

It was understandable that George III should not want to put the Treasury in the hands of a compulsive gambler like Charles James Fox, who had gambled away a fortune of £300,000. Fox's opposition to Pitt's inspired leadership showed equally bad judgement: when he came into power in the last months of his life, he found that Napoleon never meant peace. Fox was a cult icon of the Whigs, and a hero to the irresponsible likes of A.J.P. Taylor.

I have not read Oman's seven volumes, but I do not suppose that they are a monument of Whig prejudice. During years he travelled all over Spain and Portugal, visiting the battlefields, with his special interest in them and the record (and records) of the regiments engaged. Once he had been confronted in the north of Spain by an old virago's diatribe against Isabella – when he realised that it was not meant for Spain's Queen Isabella, but for our Elizabeth I.

Country people are apt to nurse long memories. Oman was well into the folklore too. At college gaudies he would sing the war songs about 'the bloody Albuera', and the sieges of Badajoz and Ciudad Rodrigo. To me he was a living monument of history. He had witnessed Napoleon III and the Empress Eugénie on the terrace of the Tuileries, watching the Prince Imperial drilling his squad of a hundred cadets – the Emperor already failing and crumpled up, Eugénie radiant in a zebra-striped crinoline. Then, after the disastrous Franco-Prussian War, Oman saw the deleterious trio – William I, Moltke and Bismarck – make their victorious entry abreast into Frankfurt, Prussians not much welcomed there.

Oman was a happy euphoric character who got a good deal of fun out of being an historian. Richard Pares described his expression on the portrait in our common room as the 'rogue-elephant look' on his face. At Lanercost priory he had seen a Roman legionary's memorial tablet to his young wife, Titilina Pusita. 'Did he call her Titty Puss?' he wondered.

He happened to be present at scenes worth recording, and the historian conscientiously recorded them. Mr Gladstone's stay of a week in All Souls as a resident Fellow, when old and very famous (or infamous). The GOM's charm and courtesy conquered lifelong political opponents, and he clearly enjoyed himself. Fellows were struck by the old-fashioned conservative tastes of the Radical Home Ruler.

He didn't want women, let alone women's colleges, at Oxford. He deplored lack of discipline. The young men should attend Chapel services regularly – as he did, reading the Lesson in that melodious voice that had seduced so many audiences, right back to the Reform Bill. He did not much care for Lord Grey or Palmerston, but spoke up warmly for Cobden. He clearly disliked Disraeli, and thought him a hypocrite. The Fellows decided that Gladstone, after all, was not, but sincere in spite of all his tergiversations and changes of front. Perhaps, rather, he took himself in. All the same, Trevelyan, who often came down for those weekends, told me that the Senior Fellows really thought the GOM phoney. Naturally enough: they were Liberal Unionists.

Oman told me that we in our time had no idea of the pinnacles on which the Victorians placed their great men. Hence the shock when Froude wrote honestly about Carlyle and the unhappiness of Mrs Carlyle: 'I married out of ambition: he has more than fulfilled it – and I am miserable.' (She should have married Edward Irving, who could have given her what she wanted.) Actually Froude's biography rates Carlyle more highly than he deserves – as the Victorians did. They accepted his absurd pro-Germanism. Fancy his making Frederick the Great his hero, and never mentioning his well-known homosexuality. (Did he even understand it?) In its German guise Carlyle's book was hailed rapturously, and made consoling reading for Hitler's last years.

Oman had attended Froude's famous lectures as Regius Professor in his old age. He regarded them as 'the golden age of Oxford history lecturing', for they were crowded, while no one had bothered to attend Freeman's, Froude's predecessor and inveterate enemy.

*

7. Sir Charles Oman

On the threshold of Mussolini's take-over, Oman was caught in a
general strike in Venice, and had difficulty in getting away.
Northern Italy was in chaos, continual strikes, factories closed,
bomb-throwing, Communists and Fascists fighting in the
streets. Political Liberalism was at an end, parliamentary
politicians incapable of co-operating to govern, government at a
standstill. At last the Northern bourgeoisie revolted. They did
not like Mussolini, who had been a Radical Socialist, but they
decided to back his Fascists to suppress the Communists. He
then decided to throw in his lot with the bourgeoisie and take
over their leadership. Order was restored. Oman's analysis of
the situation, in class terms, makes good sense. Trevelyan's, like
all Liberal illusions in our time, was out of place.

Oman was always good for a story. One I should relate for the
benefit of future archaeologists. On All Souls property at
Stanton Harcourt were some monoliths, relics of a prehistoric
stone circle. During the Second War these were buried to
construct an airfield, their whereabouts forgotten. A find awaits
some future dig!

There was an extaordinary roll-call of eccentric Victorian
dons, one or two of whom he could recall. One Fellow of Corpus
went off his head, but recovered his sanity by the mediation of St
Cuthbert. So the fool actually changed his name by deed-poll,
and went thereafter by the name of Cuthbert Shields. At
Magdalen a life-Fellow nailed his rooms up, leaving an opening
in his door for his meals to be passed in and slops out. Himself
within spent his time agreeably carving the wood panelling of
his walls. A set of rooms at Pembroke had a more sinister
memory – two, if not three, suicides in succession. I forget the
details.

Oman trusted so much to his marvellous memory that
sometimes he was not quite accurate. He had a romantic Civil
War story of a young Cavalier officer being shot against the city
wall in Merton Fields. The basis of this story was true. The
Cavalier had gone out of Oxford to be married at a country house
on the border with Parliamentary forces. The house was full for
the wedding, bridal party, friends with their ladies, when it was
surrounded by enemy troops. Instead of defending the house and

fighting it out the Cavalier bridegroom surrendered it on terms. For this he *was* executed, but in Oxford Castle, not against the city wall.

Oman thought the story would make a good film, as no doubt it would. But the old Professor was not enough of a Hollywood figure to bring that off. My Oxford contemporary, Graham Greene, could have done, but he knew no history, and would have mixed it up with his bogus religiosity – perhaps made the young Cavalier a Catholic, framed by Protestants, etc.

He continued to write, even in the House of Commons, where he was out of place (they called him 'Stone Age man' – but at least he was not an Appeaser). He wrote a standard book on the Coinage of England, besides a book of his historic memories, and even one on the Writing of History. On that subject he had no use for theorising, or any interest in abstract concepts: he called that sort of thing, not unkindly, 'the Wider Oneness'. I think that this referred to the League of Nations, and Liberal illusions about peace (with a militant Germany, Hitler and Mussolini in the wings!). We cannot now say that he was wrong – or, alas, out of date in this tragic century.

He left us two personal legacies in his historically trained son and daughter. The younger Oman became our leading expert on the history of silver. I was thrilled when he told me that the largest deposit of Elizabethan silver was in the Kremlin: the result of the Elizabethans being first to open up trade with Russia by the northern sea-routes.*

Carola Oman wrote several good historical biographies. One of Charles I's Queen, Henrietta Maria – a fatal liability to him; and the standard biography of Sir John Moore – there shone out her father's interest in military history and the Peninsular War. She also wrote the finest biography of Nelson, if too long at some nine hundred pages. I was touched to tears by Nelson's end and

---

* cf. my *The Expansion of Elizabethan England*, chap 5.

– the last entry in the Journal the night before Trafalgar. Next day after the battle, when stern Collingwood came up on deck from down below, and the seamen saw that the Admiral was crying, they knew that Nelson was dead, and sat about and wept too. A *Punch* review, noticing a quote from me, said that the book was so long that even Dr Rowse's tears had time to dry up.

Oman gave me his book *On the Writing of History*, a few days after the Second German War broke out, September 1939. The most significant piece was 'A Plea for Military History'. It began with a devastating exposure of Machiavelli's mistaken notions of military matters; as a civilian he had got it all wrong. 'He thought that fire-arms were to continue negligible, that the day of cavalry in battle was quite over, and that infantry was going to continue in very large units, using neither pike nor arquebus, but short weapons for close combat like the sword of the ancient Roman legionary.' The doctrinaire was wrong on every count.

This should have been a salutary warning for us of the younger generation who discounted military affairs, and the part played by war in history. As Oman pointed out, disgust with the horrors of war was no reason for ignoring the factor of war in the annals of mankind. He cited the Liberal optimism of J.R. Green as a case in point. He was reflecting, all unaware, the exceptional security that Britain enjoyed in the nineteenth century. Actually, we owed it to Trafalgar and Waterloo.

The only war which Green allowed to have affected English society and English government was the so-called 'Hundred Years War' with France – really a succession of contests between those two branches of medieval military aristocracy, the Anglo-Norman and the French, both French-speaking. Oman condemned 'the miserable Hundred Years War' as 'this vain and immoral venture'.

So, proper appreciation of the intellectual importance of the subject does not imply indiscriminate moral approval – though some wars may be justified. For self-preservation or liberation from tyranny; for example, the liberation of Europe from the evil of Nazi Germany, or of European peoples demanding self-determination from Napoleon.

This issue came up in a fascinating argument with General

53

Montgomery on the eve of the liberation of Europe in 1944. He was down in Cornwall for last discussions with Eisenhower before D-Day. I was asked to meet this remarkable figure, back from his victories in North Africa.

He put the question to me, as an historian, if all wars were to be thought bad. I said No, and instanced the struggle of the Dutch – aided by our Elizabethans – to free themselves from Spanish dominion. This had had the result of bringing into existence one of the most creative of modern nations. Even from our terrible experience of the First World War much new medical knowledge had been gained. Montgomery said that modern techniques of warfare meant far fewer casualties. I do not remember mentioning the tremendous casualties of the Russo-German conflict then going on. But I did cite the heavy casualties from modern area-bombing.

Montgomery simply repeated, 'My experience tells me ...' He was thinking of North Africa. I did not pursue the matter further. It was not his forte to win an historical argument, but to win battles. And I prayed that all might go well in the tremendous test immediately upon us. No one at the time, not even he, knew of the nuclear bomb and its potentialities.

CHAPTER 8

A.H.M. Jones

A.H.M. Jones was the foremost Roman historian of his time, one of the best that this country has ever produced, quite the equal of J.B. Bury. Professor Liebeschütz equates him with Mommsen.

I may be wrong, but I regarded him as a recruit of mine to the University Labour Club, where he succeeded me as Chairman. He remained always a man of the Left, though wasting no time on politics, while I in time moved on out of the slough. He was a Fellow of All Souls for twenty years, 1926–46, though we saw little of him, for he married very early and was tied down to family life with a dominating spouse. He was exceedingly academic, taking no interest in anything except his work, of which he accomplished a prodigious amount.

This meant that he was a dull man. I hardly ever heard him say anything of interest, except once when he expressed a strong dislike of Julius Caesar. This surprised me, but it fitted in with his unchanging Leftist views. He disapproved of Caesar's displacing the Senate's authority. But, surely, Senatorial government was already breaking down, and showing itself unfit to govern an empire. Caesar was caught in the transition from Republic to Principate eventually established by Augustus. Moreover, on the personal side, if Caesar had not crossed the Rubicon with his army to defend himself, the Senate would have laid him low. As a modern historian I see his case as rather like Cromwell's in 1649, or Bolingbroke's in 1399. Self-preservation concentrates a man's mind wonderfully.

Jones remained unconvinced by these considerations. He was both consistent and obstinate. He was however flattered when I said that he gave the impression of being a Wykehamist rather than a Cheltonian. He was devoted to New College, and as an undergraduate to its medieval architecture, and he began archaeologising there. He and Warden Smith wanted to replace the pleasant sash-windows in the front quad with pseudo-medieval tracery. Fortunately this was turned down, but as a concession *one* window was thus traceried next the Hall staircase. We may regard it as a memorial to Jones.

He next went archaeologising in Constantinople, digging up the Hippodrome under the aegis of the crude Stanley Casson. Casson was the victim of an unrecorded Spoonerism. Meeting him in the garden Warden Spooner said, 'I hope you will come to the dinner we are giving for our new Fellow Mr Casson.' To which the new Fellow replied, 'But I am Casson!' Spooner: 'Never mind. Come all the same.'

I remember Jones returning from his dig at Jerash, astonished to have found the strata of five or six successive civilisations. It must be one of the most ancient sites in the world, at the crossroads between Egypt and Mesopotamia.

His writing career began with a readable book on a fascinating theme, the murderous Biblical family, *The Herods of Judea*. I read it with avidity. He was already well into a large work on the Cities of the Eastern Roman Empire. He was much influenced by the big work of the *émigré* Russian Rostovtsev's *Social and Economic History of the Roman Empire*, which we all read. We were also disappointed that Oxford did not make room for him but allowed him to escape to America.

Another influence at the time was that of Spengler's *Decline of the West*. This was the major influence in starting Arnold Toynbee on his long trek, A Study of History in twelve volumes. I disapproved of Spengler who, in typical German fashion, portrayed civilisations as entities having discernible lives, while unable to see that it is individuals who are born and breathe, live and die. Nor did I care for Toynbee's attempt to sociologise history, under a law of Challenge and Response. He apparently never noticed that a young Fellow of All Souls, G.F. Hudson, put paid to that thesis in a footnote to the first volume.

Nor was Jones a disciple of Rostovtsev; he took a line of his own, and became a finer historian. Professor Liebeschütz tells us that 'Rostovtsev saw the crisis of the 3rd century AD, as a consequence of resentment by the peasantry of what he calls bourgeois civilisation. Jones saw the same conflict from the peasants' point of view. In his reconstruction, exploitation of the peasantry led not to violent reaction but to apathy and demographic decline.'

There was also a difference of approach and method. Where Rostovtsev was a generaliser, of the Continental type, always open to theorising and theses, Jones was an exponent of more reliable empiricism and adherence to fact. He made it 'a matter of high, even moral, principle to set out the evidence fully and clearly, so that the reader could assess the argument at every stage.'

Thus he never entered into any controversy, so beloved of lesser academics. He became an absolute master of evidence of every kind, in his own work sticking restrictedly to the evidence, taking no notice of the latest bright theories as to this or that. Though he wrote with exemplary clarity, this may have made for a certain lack of shine, for his dominant interests were administration, jurisdiction, law. As against Rostovtsev he was able to show that Roman cities were not mainly centres of trade and commerce, but administrative and social centres, eating up the produce of the countryside.

Hence, we modernists can see for ourselves, the speedy withering of the towns in Roman Britain with the withdrawal of the legions. The *DNB* concludes that he 'could hardly have written so much and over so wide a range from personal scrutiny of the evidence, if he had not restricted himself as he did. His practice resembled that of Fustel de Coulanges, whom he rivalled in the range of his knowledge, which no contemporary historian of antiquity equalled.'

I was lucky to be able to corral so eminent an historian on my doorstep for my Series, for which he wrote *Constantine and the Conversion of Europe*. Though he was a devout rationalist and unbeliever, he was not one to carry his personal prejudice into his reading of history. He held that Constantine was genuine in his religious belief. Of course that could well consort with political convenience. I am amused by such ready coincidences in the human frame. But I could not persuade him to follow up with a St Paul (not my favourite saint) and the Rise of Christianity; that would have got Jones into too much trouble with the credulous.

He did not concern himself much with the hoary old subject of the Fall of the Roman Empire. I have long held the view that it was far more remarkable that it should have lasted so long as it did, giving relative peace and security over so large an area. Especially when one considers the endless tides and turns in human affairs, the quick chops and changes. Apparently this was Jones's view. 'He was much more interested to explain how it was kept going for so long. He placed principal responsibility for the fall of the Western Empire on barbarian invaders, and argued that the survival of the East was to a significant extent due to the efforts of its bureaucracy.' It is a judgement in character with the man. Professor Liebeschütz sums up: 'Jones did for the Later Empire what Mommsen had done for the Republic. It is a safe prophecy that both books will be consulted as long as Ancient History is studied at universities. The *Later Roman Empire* is indeed a *monumentum aere perennius*.'

Ancient History was much to the fore at Oxford at that blissful time. Hugh Last, whom I hardly knew, was a good Roman historian. A rather nasty man, a reactionary, he opposed the study of anthropology on the ground that 'an acquaintance with the habits of savages is not an education'. He made a point, for the subject is not one for undergraduates, but for graduate research. He rather persecuted the nice modest New Zealander, Ronald Syme, who won more fame. There was an uncritical cult of his book, *The Roman Revolution*. This detailed work applied methods comparable to Namier's to the Caesarean period and the Civil War that followed upon Caesar's assassination. In the whole book not a word is spoken in favour of Caesar's heir, Octavius, who became the Emperor Augustus. He is consistently written down. I am no Roman historian, but feel sure that that cannot be right.

CHAPTER 9

Sir Maurice Powicke

Someone said of F.M. Powicke that he had genius but not first-rate ability. There was something in this. He had a streak of genius, intellectual fastidiousness, and charm, rather than power – unlike so many forceful characters in the field. He made his mole-like way by quasi-religious dedication to the Middle Ages – an appropriate attitude to the subject. In consequence his life-work left a distinguished monument to it.

He began with a thesis on *The Loss of Normandy* – which a misprint advertised as the 'Lass' of Normandy. His chosen field was the thirteenth century, to which he remained faithful, branching out occasionally backward and forward, never trespassing very far. He was rather a medieval monk in type, very sympathetic to medieval religion, though of Nonconformist parentage. His father, a minister, had written books about their sects.

Powicke was an authority on medieval universities and did much work in revising and updating Rashdall's standard work on the subject. He was attuned to the homely aspects of early college life, and enjoyed frequenting Merton, model of the first foundations at Oxford (and of Peterhouse at Cambridge). He was an *aficionado* of the ancient barn-like library there, and carried out a labour of love on its rare collection of medieval books.

Meanwhile, digging into his special field, he produced an impressive *magnum opus, King Henry III and the Lord Edward*, in two stout volumes. Henry III was an adventurous erratic ruler, but we must give him credit as an aesthete of refined French taste – to whom we owe Westminster Abbey, most French of our great churches. Was Simon de Montfort a hero to

59

Powicke, as to many Victorian Liberals – in spite of the record of the family in the cruel and crazy persecution of the Albigensians? I suggested to Powicke what a fascinating book their story would make. He lit up at this, and said that it would carry one all the way from the Scottish Border through France and Italy to the Eastern Mediterranean. But he did not bite. I think he was not particularly attracted to family history (as I am) – the effective unit of social and much political history.

A central theme of the late thirteenth century was the calling of parliaments. The origin of this institution became the subject of embattled controversy among specialists with no historical imagination and little understanding of how things come about in human affairs. Powicke wasted no time on this superfluous battleground. 'I have never been able to see the gradual emergence of the parliamentary process, and the knights and burgesses as active elements in it, as the outcome of clearcut administrative acts, like the invention of a new Chancery writ.' How sensible this was, and what a tactful way of bypassing a lot of technical palaver. It showed the common-sense realism, under Powicke's liberal idealism. Of course the process was a natural part of the rise of the English middle class. It was natural, since they were already dominant in most shires and towns, that government should call them up for consultation and co-operation at times of crisis or of urgent financial need.

Powicke was a genuine liberal in all respects. Once I argued with him that there was now no need for a Liberal Party encumbering the ground. There could never be a Liberal government again – no need for it, since both parties were essentially liberal today: one was either Conservative or Labour. Powicke, an honest and sincere man, replied, 'I dare say you are right. But it is very difficult when you have been a lifelong Liberal.' That probably spoke for a good many *bien pensant* persons at the time; but that was no excuse for condemning themselves to political nullity, when they could have made a positive contribution to the political life of the time. They should have joined up with the Labour Party to make an *effective* Opposition to the disastrous course of Baldwin and Chamberlain, 1931–39.

9. Sir Maurice Powicke

To the new Oxford History of England Powicke contributed the volume on his period, *The Thirteenth Century, 1216–1307*, from Magna Carta (the significance of which has been distorted and magnified in populist politics) to the accession of bored, incompetent, unfortunate Edward II. Being a medieval king was rather like walking the gangplank, apt to be a *sauve qui peut*. All that need be said of this solid textbook is that it is the most distinguished of the medieval volumes in the series.

All the while Powicke was fertile in essays, articles, lectures, contributions to periodicals, even to his favourite *Manchester Guardian*. These were much dispersed and sometimes hard to come by. I happened to be advising the Odham's Newspaper combine, which was making a venture into the field of publishing books. To them I suggested a volume bringing together some of these essays. They couldn't believe that such a book would appeal, and were surprised when it sold well. So was Powicke. The old innocent asked the University Press how much was in his account, and received the answer – £25. The title I thought up, *Ways of Medieval Life and Thought*, made him several hundred pounds. Surprised and pleased, he followed it up with another collection, *Modern Historians and the Study of History*.

The outstanding success in this venture was my suggestion (somewhat ungratefully taken up) of a biography of Hitler by Alan Bullock. It made the foundation of his subsequent writing career. The newspaper tycoons had no idea, except of producing best-sellers, like rabbits out of a hat. Shortly I got tired of being frustrated over my suggestions of modest, but practicable, books of good sound history. So we gave up by mutual agreement.

Those two books show Powicke at his most appealing – he wrote like an angel. 'Aelred of Rievaux' is a study of a monk and monastic friendship, tender and touching. Few historians there are of whom one could use such epithets. Powicke had an intimate sympathy with monks and the religious life. He also was the teller of a good story. I was charmed when he told me of the medieval priest who had been dancing and singing all night

61

– when he came to say Mass early next morning, instead of the Latin words of the canon, he found himself intoning, 'Sweet leman, my love.' It is pure Chaucer.

He had a gentle, rather sideways sense of humour. He reminds us that Guy de Montfort 'earned a most uncomfortahble position in Dante's *Inferno*, when he murdered his cousin, Henry of Almaine, in an Italian church.' At Oriel Provost Ross was a stiff upright Scot of surpassing rectitude, while the Senior Tutor, Marcus Niebuhr Todd, was so virtuous as to be hopelessly 'gone to the good'. When Ross produced his book, *The Right and the Good*, Lady Powicke said that she couldn't see any difference, she thought they were the same thing. Her husband explained: 'That is because you are not a member of Oriel senior Common Room. If you were, you would know that Ross is always Right, and Todd is always Good – and they are by no means the same thing.'

The gloss upon this joke is that it is so revealing of Powicke. He did not explain the difference in abstruse abstractions, but in recognisable personal terms.

Those two volumes of essays give one a complete insight into Powicke's qualities as an historian: they should be reprinted. He brought together several collections of lectures, on Christianity and History, one on the Reformation. I admired his phrase on the 'self-controlled statesmanship' of Elizabeth I – true for her, true for him: it speaks volumes on the character of her rule, guided as it was by Burghley.

One of these volumes, *Medieval England*, appealed specially to me, for it portrayed its social structure in terms of class – baronage, knightage, burghers, etc. Oddly enough the foundation of the structure was missing: the peasants upon whom, and the surplus their labour created, it all rested. (Marx would not have left them out – nor I.) Powicke's view of medieval society was somewhat idealised, not wholly in keeping with the facts of human nature. He omitted the squalor and the brutality.

One minor quibble here is his uncertainty about paragraphing – true for so many writers (notably for Lytton Strachey whom one would have expected to be expert). There should be a paragraph break on every page at least, for the benefit of the reader, who can hardly concentrate for more. An imperceptive academic, like E.K. Chambers, will go on for pages unnoticing – and Powicke was a perceptive person.

He was a professional scholar, in touch with universities and fellow scholars around the compass. He had a congenial feeling for the history of universities – most characteristic creation of the Middle Ages; he regarded their scholars as united in an international fellowship. He wrote beautifully, not uncritically, of Oxford and by his life's work and concentration – he *lived* history and the life of scholarship – he made Oxford during his time the chief European centre of medieval scholarship.

He knew the German authorities, but his affiliations were with Paris and French scholars – a more civilised and civilising influence, particularly appropriate for the thirteenth century: 'that century which, I imagine, we all feel to be medieval as no other time, not even the more vigorous and formative century which preceded it.' (I think of them visually – Durham Cathedral for the one, Salisbury for the other.) Powicke's admiration was for such scholars as Bémont, Léopold Delisle, above all the great Pirenne, whose *Histoire de Belgique*, in five volumes, is a noble monument in our ignoble time. Properly praised by German scholars, it was condemned by German patriots as a partisan piece of 'Belgian imperialism'! The great historian was hustled off to confinement in Germany during the war of 1914–18, as the leading Dutch historian, Huizinga, was in their later war of 1939–45. Then the French medievalist of genius, Marc Bloch, as a Jew was shot by the barbarians.

Powicke was an inspired scholar. Some of the poetry that occasionally surfaces in his prose qualifies him for an anthology of the finest prose in our time. His fundamental quality was sensitiveness, not only aesthetic but moral, perhaps we may say even spiritual.

I have an humiliating confession to make. Though I knew him rather well over the years, I was not appreciative of the religious element deep down in him, or the element of greatness in the little man. His exceptional antennae intuited the tragedy of our time, the break from the security and certainties of the nineteenth century. 'How innocent, how ignorant, how safe a boy

was then, as he sat and read and read in his father's library.
...The cause of this confidence was the belief that man had
become adequate to his surroundings. That belief has been
shattered.' In other words, things have gone beyond the human
scale, out of control – notably the population of the planet itself,
and the exploitation of its resources unprecedented in previous
history. For all Powicke's dedication to the minutiae of research,
he had a philosophical perspective. 'The history of man as a
thinking animal occupies a minute period of time on a tiny
planet in an unmeasurable universe.' In the confusion and
dismay of our time 'some scholars have retreated into their
laboratories and repudiate any responsibility.' (That speaks for
me.)

Powicke accepted the responsibility of a public post and
continued to hope, though he agreed with Tolstoy's too sweeping
'Once admit that human life can be guided by reason, and all
possibility of life is annihilated.' I do not agree. If men –
irrational as they are in the mass – are not guided by reason,
then by what? Powicke was, like his medievals, a religious man:
he found consolation, perhaps guidance, in the life of spirit, in
the horrors of our *naufragantis saeculi*.

CHAPTER 10

K.B. McFarlane

It is probable that no one has ever known so much about fifteenth century England as McFarlane, since those days. And he was the most devoted master of medieval research in our time at Oxford. We were exact contemporaries, and for years he was my closest friend. The best tutor in the History School, why was he not better known to the outside world?

The answer was that he would not – could not – finish his books. J.P. Cooper, his pupil (and mine in political theory), wrote, 'He liked plans and beginnings, but failed to finish the important projects which he began. For him the pleasures and rewards of acquiring knowledge dangerously outweighed those of publishing it.'

It happened by luck that I was the only person who succeeded in extracting a book from him. This was a book for my Series, *Men and Their Times*. The key idea was that of a biography which should so approach, or open out, the significant subject to which the life essentially contributed. McFarlane was so contrarious that I hardly dared to suggest a subject to him. He suggested his own – Wyclif: what more significant for the later Middle Ages, and the break-up ultimately heralding Protestantism and the Reformation? He would *not* have that in the title – perhaps it savoured too much of popular appeal. It *had* to be *Wyclif and the Beginning of Nonconformity* – too much of a mouthful.

His pedantic point was that the Reformation, when it came about, was imposed by the state from above. We all know that, and Henry VIII's part in it. But other streams contributed: the Lutheran influence coming from abroad (Cranmer), the movement for Reform, the Cambridge intellectuals (Erasmus), the demand for the Bible in England and vernacular services (Tyndale). This coincided with a considerable popular movement from below, coming from the Lollards, which had never been extinguished. In point of fact Lollards were still being unearthed and persecuted by the bishops in Henry VIII's reign, right up to the Reformation.

Never mind, I had to take what I got – the most distinctive book in my Series, with much new and original research in it. This was a bonus and quite unexpected. So also was McFarlane's attitude to the subject. He was a man of the Left. But the book's sympathy was all for the authoritarian Archbishop Arundel, bent on keeping order in the nursery and suppressing the Wyclifite movement at Oxford.

I am all in favour of keeping order in the nursery. But hadn't Wyclif been largely right intellectually – in his demand for reform in the Church, cutting down luxuriant extravagance, the waste on nunneries and monasteries, pilgrimages, the worship of the saints? Or even further – the claims of Papal dominion, the doctrines it rested upon, nonsensical metaphysical assumptions, transubstantiation, sainthood, the claims of the clerical estate; the intervention of intermediaries between the Christian and his God? Wyclif was evidently a Puritan, and he *was* a forerunner of the Reformation.

He was also, as McFarlane depicted him, rather specially an academic trouble-maker. And shortly I realised whom he had in mind for this part – his troublesome colleague, A.J.P. Taylor. (We had both had a hand in bringing him back from Manchester, alas, and he gave his senior colleague constant trouble.)

J.P. Cooper (who was another – later on at All Souls) realised that my early attachment to Marxist thought was a formative influence on McFarlane's work. He pin-points that 'most of the quotations from Marx [in a 1929 paper] come from an essay by A.L. Rowse'. This was my early booklet *On History*, which served as a blueprint for much of my later work. Cooper has to subtract, 'while he may not have gone all the way with Rowse's later claim that "Marxism is the intellectual system which had *relevance* and *significance* in modern conditions." '

Well, one may still ask whether any other has had more, in the twentieth century? I was above all influenced by Marx's views on history – I was never a Communist, unlike Taylor (briefly) and Christopher Hill (for years). Marx analysed society in terms of class, class interest, and class conflict – as does Aristotle in his *Politics*. The bulk of McFarlane's work, significantly, was devoted to research into *The Nobility of Later Medieval England* (edited by Cooper), and *Lancastrian Kings and Lollard Knights* (edited by G.L. Harriss).

It was extraordinary that MacFarlane did not publish these works himself, for in my view they are masterly. We all considered that he suffered from a writing-block – as sometimes he did. But that was not it. He was writing away, then rewriting, actually writing out lectures at full length, and giving papers to various societies. Above all, he was pursuing research: that was his passion. And he was a perfectionist. Over his desk, in that familiar room at Magdalen, bursting with books and flowers (cats and keys on the mantelpiece), there should have been posted the French proverb, 'The best is the enemy of the good.'

Nor did he heed the warning that Richard Pares gave (from his own sad experience): 'Of the making of a book there must some time come an end.' Reasonably enough there is no end to research: one is always finding something later that might, perhaps should, be in the book. No matter: the account must be closed, if only temporarily, and the book should be an organic whole. Neither McFarlane nor Pares would learn from me: they were the professionals. They seemed to care more for research than for writing up the results. I too loved research, but knew that it should be subordinated to the writing of history as an art. Though we were close friends, they did not share my view. Why not? I could have taught them a thing or two about writing.

The upshot was that, when McFarlane died, his work uncompleted, it remained for his pupils to collect it together, much of it from manuscript, in three volumes. I regard them as masterly. Also, rather paradoxically, he wrote well, concisely and firmly, no *tendresse* (unlike Powicke): a technician, critical of everybody; not bound by previous convention, full of his own insights. And, in fact, he proved readable. Why then did he not give us the chance of reading him? He was rather close, and confined himself to his disciples. He virtually headed a little school of his own, at least a *cénacle*. He worked on his own, was completely independent, and I do not remember his expressing an admiration for anybody, except for Maitland.

All his work was devoted to the analysis, and sometimes description, of late medieval English society. Unlike Powicke, he was not European in outlook, and he had no use for religion. That must be regarded as a defect, perhaps a serious failing, in a medievalist. His outlook was entirely secular, rationalist, with no illusions whatever, and more than a touch of cynicism. He understood human beings very well, and always saw through their pretences. He could admire a great man when he, as so rarely, found one – Henry V, for example, or, as I recall, William the Marshal.

His name came to be associated with the concept of 'Bastard Feudalism', about which he published articles. This raised a certain amount of dust in controversy, primarily because of its being thought of in too categorical terms. History is fluid, as Powicke held, always in flux, never at a close. So bounds should not be set too hard, or conceived too technically. McFarlane constricted himself (and his disciples) here.

Later medieval society – late fourteenth annd fifteenth centuries, from the impact of the devastating European plague, the Black Death onwards – saw a gradual change from servile tenures in pure terms of land and service to more mobile relationships, i.e. away from *echt* Feudalism. Why call the quite natural transition 'Bastard'?

The barons and richer knights came to have their retinues – more mobile than under the static relationships of early feudalism (as in Domesday Book) – held together by indentures. They were for service in peace as well as in war, for life, or for a term of years, with regular fees according to scale. This appears a natural development of society as it became richer, more complex and diversified, particularly with the increasing use of money. I see the cash-nexus as developing along with the features of early capitalism. Why make such a fuss about it, as the technicians did, drawing ever finer distinctions and constructing their catagories, going into minutiae less than enlightening as to the reality and muddle of life. McFarlane himself got rather bogged down in this, but fortunately not entirely. He had too much sense of life and reality, unlike some of the dry-as-dust camp-followers.

He was far from dry-as-dust, though the technician sometimes allowed technique to become an end in itself, as I never would. He had begun his career with a doctoral thesis on the Finances of 'the Rich Cardinal', Beaufort. He never concluded this for, as he told me, they simply did not add up. Try adding up a column in Roman numerals – no wonder the sums are often inaccurate. Out of this frustrated endeavour came two articles, one on the early crisis in Beaufort's life. He overreached himself in getting Pope Martin V to make him legate *a latere* in England for life. Henry V was not standing that from his uncle: it threatened the liberties of the English Church, as Archbishop Chichele warned the King, who was determined to be master in his own house. The episode reads like a foreplay of Henry VIII's treatment of Wolsey.

The second article reveals Beaufort on his death-bed, still worrying about his money. If, in a tight spot, the bishop would vow to go on pilgrimage, 'it is consoling to find how often they ended [instead] in ecclesiastical preferment. Cardinal Beaufort's protest that he intended to die a poor man is an exquisite touch and fit introduction to a quarter of a century of successful and unscrupulous money-grubbing.' This is a harsh judgement. Beaufort, like his later kinsman, Henry VII, had the gifts of a financier. Wealth meant power, which is what politics are about. As a responsible politician the Cardinal led the party in favour of making peace with France – an end to the Hundred Years War – against the irresponsible Gloucester, who curried favour with the mob by egging on the war. Gloucester was the popular figure, the Cardinal never: but who was in the right?

Ecclesiastics were never favoured by Bruce, as they were by

Powicke – and I have a soft spot for them too. They were far more upright men thinking of the good of the country and their flock, than were the fighting fools – though I suppose human affairs, silly as they are, have need of such.

Out of McFarlane's *Nachlass* came two short books, which a pupil edited as *Lancastrian Kings* and *Lollard Knights*. The chief interest of the first is 'Henry V: a Personal Portrait'. Here Bruce rises above his technics to confirm, from the evidence, the wildness of Prince Hal's youth and his sudden conversion on becoming king, dedicating himself to his vocation. Hitherto it was not known that Shakespeare was right – much closer to the traditions and even memories of that time. Bruce, as master of the field, was not afraid to chance his arm. He concluded, 'Take him all round and Henry V was, I think, the ablest man that ever ruled England.' As for Shakespeare, he went so far as to call him the best of historians. Of course Shakespeare was the most historically minded dramatist there has ever been, with more than a third of his plays being history plays of one kind or another.

In a third volume of collected essays, *England in the Fifteenth Century*, we are given a summing-up as to the Wars of the Roses by the master. 'The broken sequence of battles, murders, executions and armed clashes beween neighbours, which we have chosen to miscall the Wars of the Roses, has long made the second half of the 15th century in England repulsive to all but the strongest stomachs.'

He was not afraid to change his mind – in fact he often did in his technical realm of 'Bastard Feudalism' and Lancastrian Finance. With the deepening of knowledge he came to see things less categorically. Lesser minds have thought up all sorts of complicated 'causes' for those wars, but in the end he came to see that they all went back to the 'inanity' of Henry VI. The breakdown of government at the centre left the way open for the conflicts for power among the rival claimants.

The *Lollard Knights* also offers new original research. The upshot of it shows that the infection of Lollardy, the spread of proto-Protestant sects and opinions, was much wider than realised. For, naturally, it was an underground movement, repressed and persecuted, hence evidence was hard to come by. It needed a dedicated researcher to smoke it out from its holes and corners.

Here is a revealing sequel to his book on Wyclif. The spread of Lollardy, its endurance and the inability of the authorities ever to root it out, offer further support to my own view that it contributed a popular element to the eventual Reformation. Sleuthing out these obscure sectaries called forth all Bruce's powers. He became an expert genealogist, always engaged in the minutiae of the *Complete Peerage*, verifying, correcting and amending its family pedigrees. He learned enough of the science of heraldry to be able to read the coats-of-arms on tombs in churches and depicted in stained glass windows.

What a corrector he was, of conventional views, historical assumptions, accepted facts! What an inquisitor – every bit of evidence was sifted, everybody corrected, many ticked off. The great Stubbs was wrong, as we all know. Then the magisterial Tout, final authority on medieval administration – Tout cannot 'conceive', something dubious, 'now it is precisely this [Tout's] thesis that seems to me incredible.' Professor Galbraith is smacked for writing that 'in the Middle Ages the members of the ruling class were in general men of arrested intellectual development.' Of course Galbraith was wrong – contrary to common sense. It did not occur to Bruce that it was a piece of middle-class inferiority complex against the aristocracy – perhaps because he himself shared it.

The American Professor Hexter gets off rather lightly. He had exposed the Leftist bias that runs all through Christopher Hill's work. Turning to the education of the medieval nobility 'for once his [Hexter's] salutary scepticism deserted him.' Professor Elton came in for stronger disapproval, not only in detail but in general. His view that Thomas Cromwell, his hero, put through an administrative revolution was summarily dismissed: all the circumstances and phenomena were present in conciliar administration already in the previous century. Elton's argument about the Treasurership in particular, 'which appears

71

to be circular, will not commend itself to those who have had cause to study the official (and unofficial) activities of such baronial Treasurers ...' and then he names them all. *He* had studied them, Elton hadn't. As for Professor Postan at Cambridge, who once had such *réclame*, McFarlane had little opinion of him, and showed how his addiction to theoretical theses led him astray from the facts.

McFarlane was wedded to facts, and loved pricking other people's bubbles. It is only fair to say that he had a psychotic tendency to do more than prick, to stab and wound – he instinctively went for the most vulnerable spot. As for poor Mr Waugh – not Evelyn, but W.T. – who was Bruce's precursor in the prosopographical researches into the minor figures of Henry IV's reign, one might construct a whole page out of his shortcomings. 'With regard to Sir John Peachey, Waugh missed the one significant fact.' When Waugh did grasp the fact, then he failed to draw the obvious conclusion. Once he was 'misled by an error of Froissart's.' Then Waugh 'needlessly complicates' something or other. And again 'the fundamental weakness of Waugh's thesis is that it is far too logical.' No doubt – but enough.

This process of endless prosopographical research might be described more recognisably as 'Namierisation': what Namier did for the eighteenth century McFarlane was doing for the fifteenth. Like Namier, he went on and on ploughing the sands until death caught him out. He left unfinished, for his pupils faithfully to put into shape, what he could perfectly well have finished himself. Even J.P. Cooper, who was bitten by the same bug, concludes, 'He was in danger of accumulating more material than he could control and an obsessive search for completeness in recovering magnates' accounts hindered their analysis.'

That was precisely what happened. The passion for research was an obsession. He was forever on the move for more, visiting county record offices, bishops' registries, lawyers' dens, libraries (private like Longleat or public like the Salt Library at Stafford, a favourite). Then there were the Public Record Office, the British Museum, Lambeth Palace Library in London. In

Oxford there were the college archives to explore, not only his own at Magdalen; and always the Bodleian to fall back on. I have known him to give up a summer vacation, free of pupils, to spend hot days in the cool shades of the Bodleian.

How much we happy few owe to him! I could fill a volume with memories of him, our walks and talks, our picnics and excursions – all the time in search of the visible evidences of the past. We walked into the country from Oxford, or went by bus or train. When Bruce got a car he would load it with the heavy county histories. And so out to cross Arnold's 'strippling Thames at Bablockhythe' – where Richard II's favourite, de Vere, crossed in December 1387, after his defeat by the Appellants at Radcot Bridge, escaping abroad to die, to Richard's intense grief. On to medieval Stanton Harcourt, with all the Harcourt tombs in the church (the historic peerage just about to become extinct). On to Minster Lovell, the ruined mansion beside the water, with its mystery of the end of the last Lord Lovell (was it at the battle of Stoke in 1487?) Then up the valley to Swinbrook, with those Fettiplaces in their bunks in the chancel – our Oman (whom Bruce called Sir Raffle Buffle) knew that that ancient family ended up with a highwayman. On to Meade Falkner's cherished Burford – he lies in the churchyard on the south side of that splendid fane.

Or it would be up along the escarpment of the Cliffe to Lincoln – the Lady Margaret's Collyweston just off the road, whence the slates came for our ancient roofs at Oxford. Thence to Helmsley, and Powicke's favourite stamping ground, the Vale of Pickering, with the ruined abbeys, Roche, Jervaulx, Rievaulx. In York Minster I have waited while Bruce worked out mathematically the vaulting of the nave, and I enjoyed the more aesthetic pleasure of studying the glorious glass.

This is not to say that he had not aesthetic interests. He was a man of cultivated tastes, a great lover of music and of flowers, especially of wild flowers. I remember his pointing out mimulus to me in a chalkstream at Ewelme, on our way to gaze upon Chaucer's granddaughter, Duchess of Suffolk, on her tomb with the little 'Rouets', or wheels, a play upon the Flemish name in her ancestry. His eye for painting – those uncompromising green eyes that missed nothing – combined with his precise dating (always definitive, as with Shakespeare problems) – led him to make an important discovery that affected the perspective of Memling's work and life. He was able to show that all previous authorities had got the dating wrong of Memling's one important English portrait, that of Sir John Dunne (or Done).*

Once we ventured on Derbyshire. We were on our way to see Tideswell, Bruce to note inscriptions on tombs of his Lancastrians, while I was taken by the brass of bishop, or perhaps suffragan, Pursglove, in full pre-Reformation vestments well on in the reign of Elizabeth. (Had the tomb been prepared long before?)

Here there was magnificent Haddon Hall, incomparably grouped above its terraces. At Chesterfield I was impressed by the serried tombs of the Foljambes, so frequently in debt to the money-lending Bess of Hardwick. On to the most exquisite of Elizabethan palaces, Hardwick itself, where we were entertained by Bess's successor, Evelyn, Dowager Duchess of Devonshire. Each summer I stayed there, the Duchess having brought over for me Bess's original accounts from Chatsworth, for me to study sitting under her portrait.

Though invited, Bruce would never return to stay there. Here was a weakness – the middle-class envy of the aristocracy, which Bruce shared with Richard Pares and E.L. Woodward at All Souls. Proletarians, like Ernest Bevin and me, did not suffer from it. Moreover, I considered it an historian's duty to explore the monuments of the past, their relics, and what was left of the way of life in them, when it was petering out to its end. Bruce was the son of a regular civil servant – so no wonder he fell for the delights of medieval administration, all those bureaucratic writs and seals, the columns of figures that would not add up. I thought that there were more satisfying ways of bringing the past to life.

That had been his intention too. He had a deep *feeling* for the past – but that was not allowed to be expressed, he thought it

---

* His editors, academics to a man, typically make nothing of this side to him, and hardly mention it.

sentimental, and reproved even sentiment. In a church somewhere up the Cherwell valley I have watched him imprint a kiss upon the brow of a knight whom he alone knew most about, lying on his tomb with the Lancastrian collar of SS. about his neck. As I have imprinted a chaste kiss upon the cold marble brow of Bess of Hardwick, in her church of All Saints, now the cathedral, at Derby.

Bruce was a repressed man, from his family background. He would not, perhaps could not, express feeling. (Powicke, released by religion, could). Bruce would have discouraged one, if he could. I never allowed him to. But I owed my life to him: he found the first-class surgeon who gave me renewal of life, when I was nearly at an end, after years of mishandling and neglect by second-rate medicos. (Is it any wonder that I have no use for the second- and third-rate in any field? – perhaps especially the field of Shakespearean study.) The only expression of feeling I ever heard from Bruce was, 'I was afraid that you might die.' Recovering life, I promised my surgeon that I would do my best to justify what I owed to him by my work. That was over fifty years ago. My one triumph has been to survive.

Since Bruce died, I never enter Addison's Walk, or hear the chime from Magdalen tower, without thinking of him. We almost always talked history, about his Middle Ages, whence I learned over and over again from him. He did not want to learn about the Tudors or even about the Elizabethan age, from me. (Why not? – a suspicious question.) This did not discourage or repress me: I went my own independent, unprofessional way, following the creed of creative fulfilment, while he procrastinated.

CHAPTER 11

A.F. Pollard

Pollard was the leading historian of the Tudor period in his generation, and he may be said to have done more for historical study in this country than anyone. For he single-handedly created the School of History in the University of London, founded the Institute of Historical Research and started the journal *History*. He created the Historical Association as a link between teachers in schools and universities. What a thruster he was – a man of power!

He learned his trade as a writer from his apprenticeship on the Dictionary of National Biography, to which he contributed some five hundred articles, mostly on the sixteenth century. He followed this up with a book on England under Protector Somerset, then rather an unexplored subject, on which he had something new to say. Particularly in regard to the Social ideas of the 'Commonwealth' men – Hales and such – with their criticism of enclosure of arable land for pasture and sheep walks, and consequent depopulation.

This meant the loss of many medieval villages – a subject which the admirable W.G. Hoskins made his own. He has guided me into the Midland countryside to see what we could find. As evening approached and the sunlight lowered one could in some places see the outline of the medieval street-plan, faint ridges, and the space where the church had been. Pollard would not have had the imagination for that sort of expedition. Hoskins was an historian with not only imagination but a vein of poetry. Pollard had none.

A Liberal of the nineteenth century school, his interest was political and constitutional, excruciatingly Parliamentarian. (I have never been an addict.) He was a dab-hand at quasi-legal minutiae (I suppose somebody must be) and catching people out. I remember a comic mare's nest which it fell to him to expose. Nobody else had seen through it. A Cambridge ecclesiastic, C.H. Smyth of Jesus College, came up with a new sect in his thesis, the Supramarians, whom nobody else had heard of or knew anything about. The Supramarians thought this, and others disagreed with their views, so the Supramarians replied with theirs. Pollard looked into the matter and spotted that the 'Supramarians' was only a Latinised form for 'overseas' men, the familiar Protestant exiles everybody knew about. A mare's nest – like the mare's nest about a non-existent 'School of Night' which those two innocent ladies, Frances Yates and Muriel Bradbrook, fell into in my Shakespeare field.

Pollard's next work was the solid volume on the second half of the Tudor age – the reigns of Edward VI, Mary and Elizabeth I – in the excellent series edited by Poole and Hunt. Pollard's was the best volume in it: political and constitutional history called out his best qualities, practical good sense, no nonsense. His was an essentially secular mind: he did not get bogged down in the nonsense of religious disputes of the time – one lot burning the other for denying stuff about transubstantiation, the other hanging the first lot for denying the Royal Supremacy.

Henry VIII performed both operations impartially, and Pollard wrote a sympathetic biography of the monster. Actually it was too sympathetic. Pollard swallowed the Henrician propaganda fabricated by Thomas Cromwell to get rid of Anne Boleyn. Henry was under the necessity to provide a male heir to the throne – and Anne failed him, as Catherine of Aragon had done before. Moreover, Anne was no submissive *Hausfrau*: she answered the King back – cleverer than he – she laughed at his tastes, the uncouth exhibitionism with which he arrayed himself. Worst of all, she told the French ambassador, Marignac – her tastes and preferences were French – that Henry was inadequate in bed. Fatal for a male chauvinist!

Anne was framed for adultery by Cromwell, who for good measure included her little pro-French circle. She had no friends otherwise, no support in the country, was unpopular and getting rid of her was a popular political move, poor woman. Henry had come to detest her, she had given him so much trouble: he may well have believed some of the dirt Cromwell fantasised, then resorted to the dangerous charge of constructive treason – Henry could believe anything that suited him (like most people).

People abroad suspected the truth. The Emperor Charles V's sister, Regent governing in the Netherlands, well acquainted with the ways of high politics, concluded, 'So they wanted to get rid of her. Only the little organist confessed.' This was the youthful musician, Smeaton, who was offered life as a bribe, then destroyed with the rest. All the others stood firm to their innocence.

Nevertheless, the coup was successful – as were Hitler's murders of June 1934. Henry was able to come back to the conservative alliance with Charles V, the commercial link with the Netherlands. All the respectable conservatives came back to Court, headed by Princess Mary and Henry's aunt, Lady Salisbury (whom Henry beheaded subsequently).

Mary Tudor sometimes professed, when it suited her, that Elizabeth was Smeaton's child, though she must have known the truth, and accepted Elizabeth as successor in the end. Elizabeth knew that her mother was innocent and had been sacrificed. It is worth noting that neither of the daughters spoke well of their father – 'whose soul God pardon', wrote Mary; and neither of them saw fit to give him a tomb at Windsor, when they could have done.

At any rate Pollard repeated the official story to me, when I was young and naturally believed it. It was many years before I went into the matter for myself and worked out the answer (as with identifying Shakespeare's dark young mistress. No reason why historical perception should not work out these problems.). Pollard's was not a perceptive mind, he was neither sensitive nor subtle; he had a strong quasi-legal faculty, very good at untangling legislative and constitutional knots – not my forte, nor my interest. This meant that he was not a good biographer, he had little perception of character. Nor was he a fastidious man.

When young I found Pollard not a genial Fellow; he was not a good *raconteur* like Oman or Warden Pember. He was rumoured to have said that the thought of the differential calculus warmed his feet in bed. He put up, agreeably enough, with the ostentatious Communism of his son Graham – affecting the proletarian, no collar or tie, red kerchief around his neck, beery unwashed squalor. I think that the Professor grew proud of his son's expertise as a bibliographer. Graham Pollard became the first in the country, responsible (with John Carter) for the famous exposure of T.J. Wise's forgeries of rare books of verse.

Some years later Pollard gave the Ford Lectures at Oxford, which made a biographical study of Wolsey, conventionally political. He hardly appreciated the genius of the great churchman, nor the tragedy of his frustrated desire for reform. Pollard was no aesthete, had no appreciation of the Renaissance, architecture or taste – and Wolsey was an extravagant patron of the arts. He was frustrated in his endeavour to hold up enclosures of arable, though he tried. He made a good beginning in suppressing a number of small nunneries and monasteries for his grand educational foundations, Christ Church (unfinished), and his school at Ipswich (hardly begun).

Hindsight tells us that he should have used his legatine authority to go further in reform, and suppress many more of the lesser monasteries. With the proceeds there could have been founded the needed dioceses that were planned at the general Dissolution later. Half of these were aborted by the appalling cost of Henry's third French war (1543–46).

One cannot forgive Henry for the destruction of Bury St Edmunds abbey – as splendid as Ely – intended as the cathedral for Suffolk; or Reading abbey for Berkshire; Osney for Oxford; perhaps Kirkstall for South Yorkshire.

Researching into the history of Parliament was much more to Pollard's taste. Victorian liberals saw Parliament as the central spine of England's constitutional evolution. This was inaccurate. Bishop Stubbs – patron saint of the Oxford History School – had devoted a volume to the 'Lancastrian Constitution' of the fifteenth century. There was no such thing – any more than the canon law of the medieval Church in England had been independent of Rome. Stubbs was wrong on both counts.

All Souls made Pollard a Fellow to support his research, as the college had supported S.R. Gardiner in his, as well as Lord Acton, who responded by wishing to bequeath us his vast library. (Too large to be absorbed by the Codrington, it was passed over to Cambridge.)

Pollard's college research took shape in his *The Evolution of Parliament*. This was challenged by the medievalists and led to boring controversy. Pollard emphasised the concept of the 'High Court of Parliament' and the legal side of its development, jurisdiction and activities. I am no constitutional historian, but could see that Pollard got this out of all proportion. In any case the backbone of constitutional evolution was to be seen in the executive, the Crown: it was not until the later eighteenth century that the powers of the Crown passed over to Parliament, and not effectively until the nineteenth century.

Pollard had no fear of controversy; he was a fighter, as his career in London University showed, where he twice stood for Parliament as a Liberal. In university affairs he enjoyed a long feud with another tough character, A.P. Newton, a good historian of early colonial enterprise.

Pollard was not a gracious man – rather odd-man-out among the grandees at All Souls in the old distinguished days. Though I was willing enough to be a Tudor disciple, he was not encouraging – in the way a greater man, Trevelyan, was. When I was approached by a London firm to edit a big new series of historical biographies,* in the enthusiasm for education with the ending of the Second German War, I hesitated and was doubtful. I asked Pollard's advice in college, but he was not interested, and gave no lead. I went over to Cambridge to consult Trevelyan, who said with brisk determination, 'Go ahead.'

By this time Pollard was a disappointed man. When Firth ceased to be Regius Professor of Modern History a medievalist was appointed to succeed him: H.W.C. Davis. After a brief

* *Teach Yourself History*, later *Men and their Times*.

tenure of the chair he died suddenly. I was strongly in favour of Pollard as the most eminent Oxford figure in the field. But he was again overlooked. The Faculty wouldn't have him. No doubt he was, as Grant Robertson would say, a *mauvais coucheur*, and he had no charm. Another medievalist was appointed, who certainly had charm, but a reputation still to make: F.M. Powicke from Manchester, an Oxford colony.

Pollard was bitterly disappointed at this second slight. He withdrew from Oxford and ceased to come to college. From London he retired to Milford-on-sea, to nurse his grievances. When offered a knighthood he refused it. However, though he is forgotten, a great deal of his work still stands – far more than that of a whole herd of knights.

CHAPTER 12

Sir John Neale

Neale was the pupil, assistant and virtually the creation of A.F. Pollard. Same subject, the Tudor period, same dominant interest – with a similar Nonconformist Liberal background – in the History of Parliament. And he succeeded to Pollard's position as head of the History School in London University and to the well-known seminar at its Institute of Historical Research.

He did not carry such heavy guns as Pollard did, but was more friendly and genial. He made up for this by his endearing enthusiasm and by the concentration of his work. Thus his four stout volumes on the Elizabethan period still stand up and have lasting value, when the productions of a man with greater gifts, such as H.A.L. Fisher, are outdated, if still readable.

Neale had real naif charm. He was a Pickwickian little figure, big bald head with exceptional brain-span, large, kind eyes, cherubic cheeks. Born in Liverpool, I suppose his name was residually Irish, and perhaps the charm came from across that Channel. However, his character was unmistakably English, like his formation and interests.

He had not had the educational advantages of the grandees, public school, Oxford or Cambridge. He taught himself to write, the hard way, with no particular gift. When he was writing his best-selling biography of Elizabeth I, he submitted it chapter by chapter to a colleague, who was a science professor, to test how it would appeal to the public.

Thus he succeeded. It had a runaway success, a little scandalous with the purest of academics, for it bore no footnotes nor boring *apparatus criticus*. Such popularity gave rise to a number of jokes. Eileen Power (some said that she stood in for touches in the portait) commented that Neale had discovered no scandal about Queen Elizabeth, but a circulation of thirty thousand. Prime Minister Baldwin, who at least read books, had a notable line in humbug. In a country house, viewing one of the innumerable beds Queen Elizabeth was said to have slept in, he breathed piously, 'Think of her there – that eagle profile!' To which some wag added, 'Thinking her eagle thoughts!'

From Oxford Kenneth Ball reviewed the book. 'Men (especially if they are professors) think they know all about women (especially if they are queens).' This cannot be so. When Elizabeth Jenkins' *Elizabeth the Great* supplied the deficiency, and her book was disconsidered by some, I rejoined that men could not feel as a female did in Elizabeth I's shoes as head of state, a ruler with all those crises, dangers, strains – and sometimes off-colour. She was tough to have survived it all, and Elizabeth Jenkins had something of her own to add to the picture.

Neale's admiring depiction of Elizabeth is fundamentally sound, particularly on the political side. There need be no partisan controversy about this remarkable ruler. Everybody in Europe at the time knew that hers was the ablest and most successful government going – even the Pope, Sixtus V, her admirer. On the personal side that shrewd man, Henri IV, made a penetrating remark. 'There are three things which nobody believes and yet are true: that I am a good Catholic, that the Archduke Ferdinand is a good general, and that the Queen of England is a virgin.'

Henry James held that 'nobody ever understands *anything*', and ordinary people cannot be expected to understand so subtle and mercurial a personality as Elizabeth's. Lytton Strachey made an impressionistic dash at it in *Elizabeth and Essex*, but Bloomsbury never understood the Elizabethan age.

Neale himself did not grasp that Anne Boleyn was innocent of the charges against her. He havered and hovered, where his master, Pollard – imperceptive as usual – had been definitely wrong. This is the only fault I have to find with the book. Neale hoped to go on to a biography of Essex, but got engulfed in

Parliamentary History instead. He talked to me about Essex and how widespread his support was in his opposition to the government. I had the feeling that he might have been more sympathetic to that light-headed aristocrat than I should have been. Essex never knew his place.

With Neale's Liberal background, and the shadow of Pollard behind him, it was natural that he should have concentrated on Parliament. He became obsessed with the institution. It may be a just criticism that, like Stubbs before him, he overestimated its constitutional importance. The real backbone of our constitutional history was, after all, the executive – the monarch governing with his Council. From most points of view Parliament is to be regarded as an *afforcement* of that, co-operating with government, not in opposition to it.

However, Neale had much that was new to offer, and one need not quarrel with its importance. For, as he pleaded, an intimate description such as he provided 'cannot be written of an earlier time. The evidence simply does not exist.' Later he wrote that from the outset of his professional career he had been 'hunting Parliamentary documents'. Here the ardent researcher – more so than Pollard – made new discoveries. Like him, Neale was adept at untying constitutional, semi-legal, knots.

In his first volume, *The Elizabethan House of Commons*, Neale was doing what Namier was doing for George III's. 'Who were these members of Parliament? To what classes of society did they belong? How did they come to be elected? How were elections conducted?...' Then, 'the House of Commons was a reflection of Elizabethan society and offers an approach to social history.'

Neale answered all these questions, and it is much to his credit – though nobody pointed it out – that the Elizabethan evidences were more difficult of access and interpretation than Namier's in the more open, less opaque, eighteenth century.

There were no less popular misconceptions to counteract. For example, the over-representations of Cornwall: forty-four MPs altogether sat for that small county, many of the 'boroughs' mere hamlets. One can hardly use the word 'representation' in these cases. People thought that – since the Duchy was important there – they were enfranchised to give added weight to the Crown in Parliament. This was simply not so. It was an obvious consequence of the Rise of the Gentry. Roosting as they were on Church lands, many of them, and making more of them with returns on land increasing, the Gentry were increasing in strength and consequence – and they wanted to sit in Parliament. Hence the demand for seats – and the smaller the 'borough' the less trouble and expense.

If proof were needed, one can see it in the fact that opposition-minded trouble-makers in the Commons, like the Wentworths – 'carpet-baggers' – sat for Cornish seats. And no one was such an oppositionist to the Crown as the Cornish Sir John Eliot was in the next generation.

It may be that Neale rather exaggerated the importance of these trouble-makers – naturally enough, for they were more loud-mouthed than normal MPs, and left more evidence. I supported his view of their trouble-making, and was anxious to see that he didn't let the Puritans have the best of the game (Dr Johnson took care that the Whig Dogs should not have the best of it). The Puritans, first and last, were nuisances, and so Elizabeth I thought. It was a great credit to her that she did not let them get away with it, as the weak James I did.

Neale and I saw eye to eye about this – though we were not colleagues we were buddies about the Elizabethan age. I did not share his preoccupation with Parliament and constitutional niceties. But I accepted that he was top-boy in our field, and profited from his expertise. Professor Elton at Cambridge did not. He contributed an ungenerous and carping biography to the DNB, and now and again indulged in sniping at our leader. It almost seems that he regarded Neale's ascendancy as a personal grievance – rather in the German academic manner.

I had reason to be grateful to Neale. When I had finished, as I thought, my biography of Sir Richard Grenville, I deliberately opted for Cape as publisher, because I wanted it to be vetted by our leading Elizabethan scholar, who was reader for that firm. Geoffrey Faber at All Souls, who had expected this piece of college research, was disappointed; but T.S. Eliot, who vetted my verse and my politics books, could never have done the necessary job on a work of historical research.

Neale characteristically took immense pains and went into every detail. He then gave me the most severe going-over I have ever received. Ill as I was, he gave me three months' more work on the book. To begin with, I had to cut ten thousand words out of it. He urged that, with a biography, one should embark on the subject as soon as one could – whereas I had put Grenville in the perspective of the family story. I was very downcast – but have never learned so much from anybody in my life, and have never looked back since. Though he did not observe that the book was well written until later, I have been able to pass on his expertise with similar operations on other people's work – especially with American academic efforts and biographies in my Series, 'Men and their Times'.

It is odd that so many people find it difficult to cut, slim and shape up their work. One would have thought that it is much easier than writing the stuff itself. Cutting is a question of intelligence and judgement.

One small return I was able to make for his kindly severity, the trouble he had taken, with me. He had a full appreciation of what Elizabeth owed to the great Lord Burghley, her prime support for forty years. Those two usually saw eye to eye about political problems, though there were occasional divergences as to policy. Neale's admiration for William Cecil did not extend to Robert Cecil, the dominant influence after his father. The little man was also something of a great man. The clue to their success was that this trio – the Queen and the two Cecils – thought in terms of the central interest of the state, as few did; and these exceptionally clever people understood each other well. There was a full politic understanding between them.

I urged this point about Robert Cecil – a more subtle personality to understand than Burghley – in various reviews. Neale took the point, and one day came up to me in the Record Office, and said that he had been going through the decisive year 1603–04. He found that Robert Cecil governed the country. But, of course: he had managed the crucial transition from Elizabeth to James, with the utmost dexterity and skill. Judgement is the *sine qua non* of political leadership.

Neale fulfilled his promise to write the Parliamentary history of the reign with two exemplary volumes. These were narrative as well as analytical. 'The narrative is very largely constructed from manuscript sources, many of which have not been printed or even used by historians, and some of which are of superlative interest ... It has therefore seemed to me an excusable ambition, if not a paramount duty, to write worthily of England's Parliament when first this can be done.' Here was enthusiasm, the somewhat naif enthusiasm that enabled him to outweigh weightier minds. When I published *Tudor Cornwall* Neale was interested to see that I had uncovered an unknown MP for him. I was not aware of it, for I was not interested in unmemorable MPs, nor their spoutings in the House of Commons. Earlier, Neale had written of the 'humdrum' of the sources. They remained humdrum to me; I was thrilled by the literature of the time, the music of the age, the architecture – those soaring palaces that expressed the daring and the fantasy of the age.

'I have treated the Queen's own speeches as sacrosanct', he wrote, 'and have quoted them in full: a concession made to no one else. They are few, but are involved and difficult.' Here again I was able to make a small contribution. He did not know the voice in which those speeches – so idiosyncratic, convoluted, sometimes evasive, sometimes minatory – were uttered. The Diary of the French ambassador, De Maisse, tells us that her voice was high, shrill, authoritarian. People's voices are some index of character, sometimes misleading. Henry VIII's voice was, surprisingly, a light tenor. Mary Tudor's, no less surprisingly, was deep, almost a bass, in which she sometimes shouted at the Council, for she could not keep it under control. Elizabeth had no difficulty.

Neale, like Pollard, had a very sharp eye for inaccuracies. When a literary scholar, G.B. Harrison, produced a booklet of Elizabeth I's Sayings, Neale simply took it to pieces in an article showing how little foundation the popular folklore had.

Succeeding the dictatorial Pollard as head of the History department at University College London, Neale was thought a bit of a dictator himself. This meant only that he ran the department efficiently. He himself told me that it gave him a duodenal ulcer. I don't wonder – one knows how tiresome academics can be and how tedious the job. Happily for me ill health and luck kept me from wasting my time in that or the snake-pit of politics. I could concentrate on writing, my real vocation.

Professor Elton queried the details of Neale's account of the critical, and rather obscure, transition from Mary's reign, and the settlement of religion. He may have been right over the quibbles involved, but the upshot was clear. Mary's reign was an unexpected hiatus. But for Edward VI's unthought-for demise the new dynamic unleashed by Henry VIII would have gone forward, with no break. Elizabeth's reign took up where her brother Edward's death had left it, in slightly more conservative, ambivalent form. The Elizabethans – Cecil, Nicholas Bacon, Matthew Parker, Elizabeth herself – were all Edwardians. We might have had an Edwardian, instead of an Elizabethan, age. But would it have been so happy?

A newspaper questioner, from the Leftist perspective of the Silly Sixties, queried why Sir John Neale and Dr Rowse were so keen on the Elizabethan age. It was one of those questions that carry their own answer – like the fool who asked Flannery O'Connor why she kept peacocks. (She did not deign to reply.)

I may say for myself that it was not Parliament that constituted the glory of the age, but the oceanic voyages, the colonisation of Virginia, the defeat of the Armada; the poetry and music of the time, the unparalleled drama; the Queen herself, and Shakespeare. It was the beginning of the crescent of England as a power in the world. I recognised with the end of the Second German War in 1945, and the loss of the Empire, that it was the end of England's great days. Henceforth the leadership of the English-speaking peoples would necessarily pass to the other side of the Atlantic.

CHAPTER 13

Garret Mattingly

Mattingly was much in my line, for his period was the sixteenth century, and he wrote the best book on the Spanish Armada. Unlike most American academics he was a good linguist, knowing both Spanish and Italian – he was properly equipped for the job. Also we were at one about American academic writing (so too the Master, Sam Morison). Standards had been deeply damaged by the cult of the German Ph.D., dominant in the later nineteenth century. Germans were thorough researchers, but in writing up the results they had little sense of proportion or relevance and piled everything in.

I had already had experience of making three or four such books publishable. It was necessary to cut them down by a third, they were so repetitive – no idea of what was relevant or irrelevant. Early on at the Huntington Library I had a telling experience with a young woman's thesis on Graham Wallas. It needed severe pruning. She was an intelligent student. At the end she said, 'I know that you are right, but if I followed your advice I should not get my Ph.D.'

Hence their inspissated unreadability. In fact, quite a lot of their productions get rewritten in publishers' offices. (Hence *their* readiness to interfere with authors' manuscripts. Compare Paul Johnson's experience, who had to tell one of them that it was the publisher's business to publish, not to write or rewrite the book. I have had a sentence inserted by an editor, in a *New York Times Book Review*, which was the complete reverse of what I think of those erratic crackpots, Leslie Hotson and Frances Yates.) When I said to Mattingly that these academics mostly do not know how to write, he replied, 'My dear Rowse, they do – *but they know it all wrong.*' Of course they have no idea that Mattingly and Morison knew how to, and set admirable models in their books – for them to follow.

Mattingly's *Defeat of the Spanish Armada* offered a model for the Politically Correct in Britain to follow. The organisers of the Quatercentenary Exhibition at the Greenwich Maritime Museum got the subject distorted. It was fairly clear that they would like to say that the Armada had *not* been defeated; and like others of their kind they had no informed understanding of Sir Francis Drake. The simple truth is that these people dislike achievement, especially patriotic achievement; for they achieve nothing much themselves, and enjoy at best second-rate, though mostly third-rate, standards. They should attend to the best authorities, not their own inspiration. The best scholars know that the Armada was thoroughly demoralised by the week's fighting in the Channel before it reached Calais, had had several losses of fine ships (including one of the finest, *Nuestra Señora del Rosario*, to Drake), and was in no condition to continue to fight. Actually a change of wind saved it from being broken up on the shoals of the Flemish, instead of later on the Irish, coast.

Mattingly gets all this right, and it is confirmed by the fascinating *Spanish* Story of the Armada by Captain Cuellar, which Froude gave us.

Mattingly followed this up with another first-class book on *Renaissance Diplomacy*. Diplomatic History has no charm for me (as with G.P. Gooch's milksop works), for it is apt to be one-track – without the further background, political, economic, social, to give it reality, the fullness of life which history demands. This is not the case with Mattingly, a fine Renaissance scholar, and so his book is a model of its kind. This is indeed the kind of model for lesser academics to follow.

This is the place to pay tribute to a comparable classic in this field, similarly overlooked: W.K. Ferguson's *The Renaissance in Historical Thought*. One of those rare books that influence one's thinking, like Huizinga's work on the Decline of the Middle

13. Garret Mattingly

Ages,* or Burckhardt's *The Civilisation of the Renaissance in Italy*. Still more, the great Sherrington's *Man on his Nature*. One never hears Ferguson's book mentioned among the conventional books recommended to students. I met Ferguson only once, at the gathering of that enormous *Kuh-handel*, the American Historical Association. Glad of the chance to tell him how much I admired his book. He knew how to write.

Another original book from that time was Francis R. Johnson's *Astronomical Thought in Renaissance England*. He was an Army man by origin, on the technical side, but professed at Stanford. He knew more than anyone about Science in Elizabethan England and the gradual reception of Copernicanism. This was his only book – I was much indebted to it for its lead – though he had written separately on mathematicians like Robert Recorde of All Souls and Thomas Digges.

A chain-smoker, who suffered badly from emphysema, he could not complete a second original project. Mattingly, another smoker, also suffered from emphysema, as did T.S. Eliot.

* *Das Herbst des Mittelalters.*

91

CHAPTER 14

R.H. Tawney

Tawney exercised the widest influence of any historian of his time, politically, socially, above all educationally. He regarded his historical work as secondary, though that had its influence too. He was the Prophet and inspirer of the Workers' Educational Association. This answered a gaping need in those days, when the school-leaving age stood at fourteen and few were the people who could get a university education.

Tawney aroused a spirit of idealism and was a noble idealist himself. He had a fine war record. He was badly wounded on the Somme, was left out in no man's land with a throat wound that would have bled him to death but for a frost at night that congealed the bleeding. Tawney regarded the approach of death without apprehension. He was a religious man, a Christian socialist, a lifelong Anglican.

He wrote a large amount of high-minded journalism for the causes he had at heart, manifestos for the Labour Party, propaganda for the coal-miners, reports of government commissions, projects for the future. Some of these activated policy; for instance, his *Secondary Education for All*. He was a prime influence on H.A.L. Fisher's Education Act of 1918.

He was deeply a populist, believing in the wisdom of the people: a doctrine that needs some qualification. He was always and in every way against the upper classes – sharing in that middle-class complex, along with middle-class illusions about the working classes, to which he did not belong. He said that he hoped before he died to see the end of the public schools. I thought that silly, we never heard such nonsense from Ernest Bevin, a sensible working man. Tawney had the Rugby-and-

Balliol outlook, a do-gooder combination that did not speak for me. He did not like the ethos of All Souls, though he used our celebrated Hovenden estate maps for his first historical work, *The Agrarian Problem of the Sixteenth Century*.

I never made much of that work. I knew the importance of the enclosure movement for pasture, sheep walks for woollen manufacture, at the expense of arable, thus depopulating villages. I was much more interested to go with W.G. Hoskins later, to explore the sites of lost medieval villages. Once, with E.L. Woodward, we went out to our village of Padbury, taking the Hovenden map of it to check the balks, ridges and headlands of ancient Elizabethan tenants, reading their names from the map. Tawney went into technicalities that were not to my taste and have since been superseded. It saves time not to swallow such tomes whole.

His key book was *The Acquisitive Society*, which expressed his whole outlook on contemporary society. He was against acquisitiveness and acquisitions. Did he never realise that the profit-motive gave the initiative, was the engine that kept industry, the whole economy, going? Strike at that – and the economy, society itself, runs down. Look at what happened under Communism in Russia! Though the argument was not so clear when Tawney wrote, I was not persuaded. I was all in favour of acquisitions, never having had any. One needed money for one's independence, freedom to choose, for the good life, a cultivated way of living. Tawney didn't need it, he came from a good old family of Oxfordshire bankers.

But he lived up to – or, rather, down to – his principles.

As a young man I was bidden down to his country cottage, Rose Cottage, near Stroud. Tawney met me, in his battered straw hat and tattered sports jacket. 'Doesn't he look like a duke?' said his wife, Beveridge's sister. She was a snob, Tawney an inverted snob. She was a hopeless housekeeper, extravagant, with a mania for spending the money on worthless trifles. In fact, to use the people's expressive phrase, she was 'scatty' (it means, scatter-brained). When I penetrated Tawney's study in Mecklenburg Square, I was amazed: not only the litter of books and papers on every chair, table or ledge, but trays with scraps of food, unwashed teacups, etc. The place can rarely have been dusted or cleaned. Tawney sat imperturbably in the midst of the mess, he didn't seem to notice the squalor.

In fact Mrs Tawney was a great trial; it was an unsatisfactory marriage: he should never have married her. Bad judgement – there was an acquisition he could have dispensed with, but never did. Too Christian, too high-minded, he put up with it, but certainly suffered from it. Such was the idealist's background. Very far from ideal, to my working-class common sense.

He and Beveridge, as young Balliol Radicals, began on the Right-wing Tory newspaper, the *Morning Post*. As leader-writers they reduced its reactionary opinions to such nonsense that their game was eventually seen through, and they were dispensed with. After the war they were united for life at the London School of Economics, Beveridge as Director, Tawney as Professor of Economic History.

As such he wrote a celebrated article on the Rise of the Gentry. He had noticed the importance which James Harington gave, in his *Oceana*, to the effect on the Gentry of their gradual acquisition of the lands of the Church. The Crown sold the last of them in 1629 – significant date. The increased economic power of the Gentry gradually led to their demand for increased political power – through their representative body, the House of Commons. As Parliament became more aggressive, the monarchy was pushed on the defensive, the eventual Civil War in the making.

To anyone with any political judgement here was a key to the Puritan Revolution – Puritanism being its ideology. However, Tawney's view was rudely challenged first by the young Trevor-Roper – though anyone with eyes to see could *see* the process. All over the country, in the churches, came the hundreds of expensive, often extravagant monuments to the Gentry, in place of the shrines of the saints. Then young Lawrence Stone rose to answer back his tutor Trevor-Roper, with another thesis on the Decline of the Aristocracy. This was also nonsense. He came to consult me. He had cited the Earl of

Kent as one of the richest of the peers, because he was not in debt. The historical *fact* was that he was one of the poorest. If you owned a mass of landed estates you could afford a mass of debt on their security. If you hadn't much land, you hadn't the security to get indebted. When I pointed this out to Stone he departed a sadder and a wiser man.

So much for historical theorising, and the controversies it gives rise to. Tawney eventually gave a halt to it as serving no useful purpose. It never had done.

His full-length book, *Religion and the Rise of Capitalism*, contributed to further controversy which had gone on abroad, notably in the sociological work of Max Weber. And how useful was that? In the Middle Ages the Catholic Church had condemned the taking of usury absolutely. But there were always ways and means of getting round the prohibition. With the Reformation Protestants, more candid, compromised. In England usury was legally condemned beyond 10 per cent. However, here too ways and means of going beyond the legal limit were found. How far did this flexibility advance the growth of a capitalist economy?

It was obviously absurd to argue that the Reformation instigated capitalism, or even that capitalism rose by it. For banks, with some of the phenomena of a money economy, were familiar in medieval Italian cities, the Bank of Genoa, etc. It is likely enough that the loosening of the authority of the Church – in so far as it had been effective – may have gone along with the increasing use of cash in the economy, not very wide even in the sixteenth century. And that is all that need have been said about it, instead of reams of controversy. History depends, as a subject, a lot on causation. There is no causal link between the Reformation and Capitalism – not even Karl Marx suggested that there was. Tawney was more familiar with Marx and Marxism than most historians, but he took it pragmatically and certainly did not swallow it whole.

He had no good words to say for Capitalism or capitalists, and, elegant stylist as he was, had a way of putting them in the wrong by sarcasm or innuendo. He noted, for instance, the 'alchemy by which a gentleman who has never seen a coal-mine distils the contents of that place of gloom into elegant chambers in London and a house in the country.' Is that the end of the matter? The returns on property were but 'a tribute paid by those who work to those who do not'. Is that all? It obviously leaves essential factors out of the account.

Tawney was not the leading economic historian in the country, though he enjoyed more influence on the more credulous section of the public than the man who was. The major economic historian was J.H. Clapham, of Cambridge, who wrote master-pieces, his Economic History of Modern Britain (three volumes), and his History of the Bank of England (two volumes). It does not appear that Clapham had much use for Tawney. Clapham realised that the Victorian age was the greatest, the most creative period in our history – in industry and trade, in colonisation and skilled leadership around the world, in building railways abroad, pushing forward irrigation and canals in India, feeding the population; in medicine and science; in literature and the arts of life. Tawney disparaged the Victorian age, the triumph of Capitalism.

He preferred the Elizabethan – which has the charm of spring, not of harvest and fulfilment, except in the drama and with Shakespeare. Even so, he reproved me for thinking too highly of the Tudors, ablest of our dynasties. He called them *'nouveaux'*. This ignores Henry VII's remarkable ancestry, directly descended from Henry V's widow, the Valois Catherine of France, and on his mother's side the able Beauforts, with their residual claim to the throne, through John of Gaunt.

When Tawney came to study the actual facts of the career of a Jacobean capitalist, Lionel Cranfield, he found himself defrauded. He had embarked on this last work of research with the aim of catching the man out and exposing him. Honest man that Tawney was, he confessed to Beveridge that he began the book 'with a prejudice against Cranfield as a capitalist on the make. I ended with a respect for a man who, without being overscrupulous in business, was in courage and public spirit head and shoulders above the awful gang of courtly sharks and toadies with whom, as a minister of the Crown, he was condemned to mix, and sacrificed his career for the service of the state.'

14. R.H. Tawney

Serve Tawney right for his career of prejudice, it should have been a lesson to him – but he was too far gone, had invested his all in the ark of his Leftism. I suspect that if he went further into his 'courtly gang of sharks and toadies' he would have found that they were not all sharks and toadies. Even the one who was most acquisitive, the Duke of Buckingham, acquired the noblest collection of works of art of anyone except Charles I himself. All their collections would have come to the nation, if they had not been sold by the Puritan Philistines to prosecute their war.

Tawney had no care for the higher things of life aesthetically: with him all was Ethics, Ethics – an elevated stratosphere I couldn't breathe in. Of course he was a good man, if not a great one. I used to doubt if the veritable cult that people made of him was altogether good for him. One observed him on platforms, sweating with sincerity, almost a halo round his head. He was not really very approachable. His friendliness, his cult of friendship, was collective rather than individual. I do not find that he was an encourager of other people's work, in the way that Trevelyan and Neale were. I once got a casual approval of my *Tudor Cornwall*; I don't think he approved of *A Cornish Childhood*, after all, a working-class work. Beatrice Webb, with her practised stethoscope on everybody, could not penetrate his reserve, or discover the extent of his religious belief. He had plenty of reason for disillusionment with his illusory hopes of the Left, in politics and society. In his last years, as hope faded, he took more and more to the consolations of religion and attendance at church.

He wrote a book on Equality. I never agreed with it, or liked Tawney's idea of life. Inequality is a fact of human nature, animal nature, all nature. As a value equality may be discounted almost arithmetically. What is the value of a murderer's or terrorist's life, who takes away human lives, compared with that of a surgeon who adds to the sum?

Or consider Tawney's proclaimed ideal of 'Fellowship', in the light of society prevailing today. In fact an equalitarian society releases more envy at every stage. Society is essentially organic, if mechanised it fails or breaks down. Some organs perform more essential services than others, are more important, must occupy a larger place in the scheme of things. To vary the image, a wall of equal pebbles will not stand up. And unequal groupings, classes for example, arise from real and essential differences of function in society. His idealism had no real, or realistic, foundation. Did he never realise this? His hopes came up against the *facts* of life.

CHAPTER 15

H.R. Trevor-Roper

Lord Dacre of Glanton must forgive me for reverting to his maiden name, under which he wrote his books and by which he is best known. His earliest and most continuous field of study has been the seventeenth century. He first appeared on this stage with a biography of Archbishop Laud. The subject was not congenial to him, for the mainspring of the Archbishop's life – for which indeed he laid it down – was his religious belief and his devotion to the Church.

Not many have been sympathetic to Laud's personality and few are those who have been able to get him quite right and do him justice. Certainly not the Puritans who drove him to death for his work for the Church. Nor their academic descendants, who continue to treat him as an innovator. Laud was born in the Elizabethan age, and regarded himself as an Elizabethan, continuing the policy of Archbishops Whitgift and Bancroft, restoring the order and decency which had lapsed under James I's negligent appointee, Archbishop Abbott.

Laud was a fine scholar, and something of an aesthete, who built the lovely Canterbury quadrangle at his old college, St John's, Oxford. He spent money collecting Oriental manuscripts for the Bodleian, which made Oxford the prime centre of Oriental scholarship for the next century. He was the most devoted, and effective, Chancellor the university has ever had.

Trevor-Roper could have been more sympathetic to the Archbishop, though it was harsh of G.N. Clark to dismiss his as a 'dud book'. The young author was out to make fun of an archbishop, counting his spoons after the banquet he gave to the King and Queen. I suspect the influence of Lytton Strachey, much in fashion at the time, and *not* a good historian. However, the book was lively and sparkling; I gave it a too favourable review.

In later years I wondered why he didn't give us a biography that we really needed, say, of the great scholar, Selden. Trevor-Roper had the classical background and some of the aptitudes – Selden's scepticism about religion and politics, for instance.

During the Second German War Trevor-Roper served in MI5, whence came the materials for *The Last Days of Hitler*, where he could not go wrong. A masterpiece of topical journalism, or contemporary history, only a first-rate intelligence could have mastered the material so effectively. A world best-seller, it made the author's fame and fortune in this field. I had only one reservation. The leading Nazis were depicted, with some superiority, as monkeys in a zoo. But this misses the point of the extent of their evil. Hitler was a genius of malignity; Göring a man of ability, an air-ace in the First War; Goebbels, the ablest propagandist of our baleful time. To write them down was, to that extent, to let these destroyers of civilisation off the hook.

Returning to his first wicket Trevor-Roper published his reflections on the seventeenth century Gentry, his contribution to the controversy he had initiated with his attack on Tawney's 'Rise of the Gentry'. The dispute enlivened academic common rooms for some time, though there was no point in it, nothing to be gained but *réclame*. We need say no more here, except to note that Tawney dismissed it, for he was wholly right, as against the young men, Trevor-Roper and his pupil, Lawrence Stone, embattled against each other.

There followed a volume of *Historical Essays* from this lively pen, the precursor of a number of such collections. For Trevor-Roper did not devote himself to constructive works of narrative history, like the greater historians, Trevelyan or Morison, but to essays, like Namier. We might say that those two were our leading historical essayists.

This went along with the fact that, to his credit, Trevor-Roper thought about historical issues, instead of being content to trample yet again well-trampled fields. He was constantly reflecting on the fashionable subject of the Crisis of the Seventeenth Century. It appears that he attempted a constructive work on this, but failed to complete it.

A collection of essays, *Religion, Reformation and Social Change*, may represent the débris of the abandoned project. I found myself in sympathy with the inflexion here. We both opt for the civilised position of an unheroic Erasmus, in the 'crisis' of the Reformation, as against the heroic, but uncongenial, Luther so much admired by Carlyle and innocents of the Victorian age.

By the same token, if one is addicted to pushing forward a thesis one is liable to go wrong – as in Trevor-Roper's next venture into a fashionable field, the European Witch Craze of the seventeenth century. I was fascinated by this brilliant essay, with its *ipse dixit* that the witch craze was 'a phenomenon of mountain country'. Was it? I stopped to reflect: it was at its hottest and most fierce in Essex, a countryside as flat as a pancake. Why? Because the county produced a furious persecutor in a leading JP, one Darcy, impelled by Puritan Bible-mania. Similarly with the outbreak in the plain of Lancashire; and again at Edinburgh, hardly mountain country, where the appalling persecution was due to Presbyterian fanaticism. The real association of witchcraft is with religion, not with 'mountain country' – as we see in these instances, or as in Germany during the Thirty Years War.* Or again, noticeably in Puritan New England.

I am not in favour of these absolute, summary statements in either history or literature: they impede, or distort, what Powicke called, more wisely, the 'flow' of history, i.e. life. History is a *plodding* subject. One plods away at research, until the accumulation of facts itself directs the shape of the story. Or, in literature, until the weight and consistency of the evidence overwhelms one as to the identity of Shakespeare's dark, half-Italian young mistress, Emilia Bassano.

* David Ogg, *Europe in the Seventeenth Century*, p. 130.

In the 1960s Trevor-Roper chimed in with the topical fascination with the Cambridge spies, spying for Stalin's Russia, to give us a booklet on *The Philby Affair*. Once more he had the advantage of his MI5 background, where they had been colleagues. Had he never suspected? What is the point of being so superior, if it does not lead one to be perceptive as to character? The one person who suspected Philby was a modest, observant diplomat – Pat Reilly, of All Souls.

And what is one to think of Graham Greene who – when Philby was revealed as traitor and apparently murderer – continued to keep in friendly touch, and visited him in Moscow to give him moral aid and comfort? Fancy people being such fools as to regard Graham Greene as a moral mentor, with his ignorant combination of Communism with Catholicism!

In the 1970s Trevor-Roper continued with essays on various aspects of his chosen seventeenth century – the *Plunder of the Arts* in the period, *Princes and Artists*, the role of patronage. I suspect that this aspect of the matter interested him more than the aesthetic – no Burckhardt. For, though an excellent stylist, one does not encounter the visual gift of a Trevelyan for landscape, or of Veronica Wedgwood for portraiture and personality.

One observes a failing as to perception of character. A detailed examination of Oliver Cromwell and his Parliaments shows him up, in a rather superior way, as a failure as politician. It was in the nature of things that Cromwell could not square the circle to achieve a constitutional Parliamentary régime. The whole basis of his rule was unconstitutional: it rested on the Army. But this did not mean that he was not a very skilful politician, extraordinarily adept to shifting circumstances. His Royalist opponents, and even Puritan supporters, knew that only too well, and called it hypocrisy. Only he could have kept the revolutionary régime going: in effect it died with him. Oliver Cromwell was, first and foremost, the politician, even in the

Army. Not to perceive that is a failure of judgement.

The question of judgement comes up again in the case of Trevor-Roper's next venture – a surprising gamble on China, of all fields. In 1976 he produced *A Hidden Life*, an account of the Chinese scholar, Sir Edmund Backhouse. This man, a recluse in Peking, was indeed a 'mystery man'. He unloaded upon the Bodleian a mass of Chinese manuscripts which were largely spurious. His claims were dubious, and he turned out to be largely an imposter.

Trevor-Roper seems to have been taken in. What on earth can have drawn him to such a subject? Backhouse was half-Cornish, through his Trelawny mother. Cornish people are inveterately suspicious, and my suspicion was that Trevor-Roper hoped for another such coup as the Hitler book which had made his name. If so, it turned out a mare's nest.

So too did his uncalled-for intervention in the case of President Kennedy's assassination. He lined up with that figure of notoriously bad judgement, Bertrand Russell, in believing – against all the evidence – that the assassination was the work of a conspiracy. Here the legal acumen of John Sparrow, Warden of All Souls, shot Hugh down.

I had already been disappointed by his questioning my work on Shakespeare. Had he studied my argument in detail? It took me years of plodding away at it, bit by bit, to get it all right. Few know that he had earlier queried whether Shakespeare wrote his own works. He was very young then, and recovered from that 'last infirmity of an [ig]noble mind'. All the same, I expected the professors and academics of the second rank to do their duty and interpret for the public the findings of the leading authority on the Elizabethan age, on the life and work of its most representative writer. Not one of them did.

Why not? They should go into the work step by step with me as I had worked it out. 'Too much like work,' said John Holloway, Cambridge professor of Eng. Lit. The Eng. Lit. professors suffered from Trade Union feeling: 'I don't read his work: he is not *in the field*,' said a third-rate academic to the Canadian writer, Hugh MacLennan. Sheer envy? Lack of perception, of persistence? No doubt all these factors enter into what is a shocking chapter in scholarship.* A sociological element enters in. This would not have happened a generation or two ago. But in contemporary demotic society with its levelling down of standards, a TV 'culture' (if that is the word for it), people simply skim over the surface and then think that they can pronounce upon it.

I have said that history is a *plodding* subject – and this should have been the lesson for Hugh to take to heart over all these subjects: the Rise of the Gentry, the Witch Craze, the Kennedy Assassination, the Chinese Imposter Backhouse, Shakespeare – and the Hitler 'Diaries'. One must *plod* – as I have done all my life – to get things right.

Trevor-Roper was made to suffer unduly – by his favourite medium, the media – for getting the Hitler Diaries wrong. Not by me – for I had observed his brilliant, but erratic, course over a long period. A better, more reliable, historian – Sir Keith Hancock – had made the point that the historian's judgement is the same as the statesman's. It is judgement that is the essential requirement. We can be misled by a brilliant surface.

* See my *Discovering Shakespeare: A Chapter in Literary History.*

CHAPTER 16

Christopher Hill

J.E.C. Hill has written so many books that he has exerted a notable influence – not so much with the public at large as with the Left, particularly with his own Leftist disciples, squirrelling away at what the ancestors of the Politically Correct of today thought. – As if the thinking of people who don't know how to think has any value! Hobbes, Milton, Selden, Clarendon, Halifax, Locke – Yes; but not that of the People at large. A great many books, and much paper, have been wasted on this stuff. Hill may be described, in the better sense of the word, as a populist historian.

For, to be fair, there is a place in history for the reactions, the demands, the grievances, the needs of the People. But the needs and demands, the opinions of government are more indispensable and more worth studying, if more difficult to grasp and understand. For government, of whatever colour, is concerned with the problems of the whole society; its point of view must be more general, the questions it faces more complex, solutions more difficult to find. That is its job. Any fool can criticise – but can he do the job?

Christopher Hill was educated at St Peter's School, York – Guy Fawkes's old school. Christopher told me that they did not celebrate Guy Fawkes' day, Gunpowder Plot, there. He has a pleasant sense of humour, as well as undoubted charm. His populism is in the Balliol tradition of Tawney, but even more in that of the missionary spirit of a Nonconformist parentage. When he was a Junior Fellow of All Souls I pointed out, perhaps needlessly, that Soviet Russia was a subject of growing significance to study. B.H. Sumner, of Balliol and All Souls, a leading historian of Russia, may have exerted more influence. Anyway, Christopher went to Russia – and swallowed the Communist Faith, hook, line and sinker.

In editing my 'Men and their Times' Series my principle was to recruit authors sympathetic to their subject, who would not sabotage it. (As one provincial professor did Francis Drake – I sabotaged *him*.) So I invited Christopher to write *Lenin and the Russian Revolution*. When it arrived I was taken aback – a work of stone-walling Stalinist orthodoxy, not a hit human. I asked him to add a few touches at least to humanise it. There was the occasion when Lenin and Trotsky were on top of a London bus together passing Westminster Abbey. 'That's *their* Westminster Abbey,' said Lenin dismissively, meaning not a shrine of the English people but a temple of the bourgeoisie.

Christopher added a few touches. With the appeal of the subject at the time his book sold best of all the Series, except for my introductory volume, *The Use of History*. Years later I asked him if he would revise the book. 'No – sick of the subject,' said he.

It had taken him a long time to arrive at that moment of truth. Not until 1956, with the Russian tanks suppressing the first shoots of liberty in Hungary, did he leave the Communist Party. It showed surprising judgement to stay with them through the whole period of Stalinism, purges and all, whatever one may think of Lenin.

In 1956 Christopher produced his best and most important book, *Economic Problems of the Church*. This is a serious work of research into the problems that afflicted the Church in the decades leading up to the Civil War. We need not accuse Christopher of undue sympathy for the Church, but there were many problems needing attention. Things had been neglected under the long primacy of Archbishop Abbott, and Laud came in with all the energy and devotion of a reformer.

He was already an elderly man, and the task he had to face was daunting. Fundamental was the impoverishment of the Church as the result of the Reformation. The vast majority of the parish clergy lived on pittances. Laud's prime aim was to improve their miserable livings. But the tithes of many of these had been granted away in 'impropriations', which had largely come into the hands of the Gentry (another factor in their Rise). Laud struggled in vain, he could never get them back, except here and there. He was always faced by the opposition of the laity, holding on to their gains.

One disadvantage of a married clergy was that bishops and deans, the higher clergy, wanted to provide for their families by forking them into the better livings at their disposal. No doubt most did their duty, some didn't. 'Men are we,' quotes Trevelyan – one is always up against the facts of ordinary human nature. Historians are apt to exaggerate grievances and complaints, charges against those in possession – naturally enough, for those are the evidences that bulk disproportionately in documents that remain. This overlooks the fact that the silent majority carry on, if not always content with their lot. This is a fair criticism that may be made of Hill's book, otherwise unexceptionable.

This is not the case with many of his later books, always biased in favour of the Puritans, Levellers, Diggers, Ranters, upholders of the *Good Old Cause*, to which he had already devoted a book which showed the way he would go. He next wrote a biography of Oliver Cromwell, which I remember liking. There was no danger of his lacking sympathy with that hero of the Puritans.

This was followed by a whole series of books, of which we may take as typical, *Puritanism and Revolution: Studies in Interpretation of the English Revolution*. In this he tells us that it is still an enigma. Is it? We have been afflicted by endless academic argy-bargy on the subject, as if revolutions are not familiar enough phenomena. They usually appear when the grip of government, of an *Ancien Régime*, is failing, and restless elements are agitating to get into power. This was the case with Charles I, also with Louis XVI in France, and with the Tsar Nicholas II in Russia; or again with the feeble Manchu dynasty in China.

What is the point of going on and on about it? I suppose it gives academics something to write about, in their pursuit of tenure.

As time went on, with successive books, Christopher went more and more into what these agitators 'thought'. Some of them, like Winstanley, whose writings he edited, were rational enough in their arguments. But the serious practical point remains: society could never have been organised on their basis of communising agriculture, like the ludicrous failure of the Diggers, taking over St George's Hill for their digging. If such experiments in social engineering have been shown to be impracticable in the twentieth century, with all its technical equipment, how utterly hopeless such attempts were in the circumstances of the seventeenth century!

By the same token they are of limited interest except perhaps to the Leftist illusionists of our time. Once more I observe that these are middle-class illusions, not shared by proletarians like myself. That book Christopher dedicated to his parents, 'who taught me most'.

In earlier books a sense of humour seems to have diverted Christopher from going too far along with them. The Ranter, John Robins, for example, 'who believed he was God Almighty, prescribed a diet of vegetables and water for his disciples, many of whom died of it.' (Only *some*, I suspect.) Another of these enlightened souls, who held 'visible and sensible communion with angels', held that 'the Saints would take over the estates of the wicked for themselves, and the wicked should be the slaves.' Here at any rate was a recognisable motive, always at work in revolutions: sheer envy of the have-nots for those who have. But what about the question of competence – who is capable of running society, and making practical social arrangements? Never academic doctrinaires. That practical man, William Shakespeare, who built up an estate for himself, observes

> They well deserve to have
> That know the surest way to get.

We need not concern ourselves with those women among the Saints – there were several of those – who thought themselves with child by the Holy Ghost and that they would give birth to the Messiah. The revelations of Ludovic Muggleton gave birth to a whole sect – as it might be Waco in Texas. I learned from

Christopher that the last of the Muggletonians died only in the 1970s. He gave far too much time to these loonies, book after book. The research he put into it was prodigious: he became doyen of the subject.

Many of the Saints, inspired by their Bible mania, were expecting, like the early Christians, the End of the World. Some of them gave an exact date for it. Christopher has an essay on these millenarian expectations. Even Milton was affected by them. Christopher wrote on *Milton and the English Revolution*. Milton was a glorious genius; but we value him for his poetry not for the theological nonsense he thought or his political nostrums. We were given yet another biography of a Puritan hero: *'A Turbulent, Seditious and Factious People'* – *John Bunyan and his Church: A Tinker and a Good Man*. Is that not the least bit humbugging? – it fetched its reward, a prize in the populist atmosphere of the refined society of today. I suppose we have all appreciated the childhood fairy-tale of *The Pilgrim's Progress*, without subscribing to the Victorian cult of Bunyan (or Bunnion). I find what Sir Charles Firth has to say about the tinker and good man quite sufficient for me.

In 1983 Hill produced, with others of his persuasion, a book on *The World of the Muggletonians*. Now was that worth it? I do not find the history of nonsense worthwhile, nor that of their foolery even amusing: to my mind the prime quality of these people is that they are so *boring*.

In a later volume of lectures he dealt with *Some Intellectual Consequences of the English Revolution*. He had been mistaken in his view that the Puritans advanced the cause of science, or even that Puritanism was propitious to the advance of scientific thought. The facts showed that scientists were more at home in the freer intellectual atmosphere of the Royalists. We have only to think of the greatest physiologist of the time, William Harvey, or indeed Christopher Wren out of that devoted Royalist stable.

Hill notices here 'the increase in men's belief in the power of the Devil' which led to the appalling persecution of 'witches' while the Puritans were in power, imputing it to 'a transitional stage'. I call this less than candid, when it was directly due to Calvinist beliefs. Anglicans like Charles I and Laud did not believe in such rubbish any more than Elizabeth I or Shakespeare had done. Hill tells us that 'after 1688 and the foundation of the Bank of England in 1694 the English constitution combined the financial advantages of a republic with the social advantages of a monarchy. It was a very happy compromise for those at the top.' It would have been more honest to add that it was happy for the country in general too.

In his last phase he was prepared to make a concession, admit a gleam of truth, in *The Experience of Defeat*. The regular argument which all the Puritans believed in, whatever their sect or other divisions, was the run of victories they had had in the Civil War. This proved to them that God was with them, that theirs was God's cause. This meant only that success proved them right. Then what about 1660, when the Restoration of the monarchy reversed it all and Puritanism was driven underground? Was God with the wicked after all? All talk in such terms is foolish. But for once Christopher had the candour to admit that the Puritans' winning argument was valueless.

The American authority of this period, J.H. Hexter, traversed the whole of Hill's work, and – to Christopher's expressed grief – condemned it of bias throughout. I believe that the charge can be justified. We must pay tribute to the enormous amount of work he accomplished – only too well recognised with prizes and awards. For, as Charles II observed of partisanship in his time, 'this nonsense suited their nonsense.' Today we have had more than enough of it.

CHAPTER 17

C.V. Wedgwood

Veronica Wedgwood was my most eminent early pupil – not the ablest: that was J.P. Cooper, a troublesome Trotskyist, who died early as a reactionary tutor at Trinity, Oxford, nothing much to show for it. Veronica wrote a great deal, and did a mass of public work. She and I kept in close touch for many years, encouraging and reviewing each other's work. I helped a bit with her arduous labours for the PEN Club – gave a large international tea-party in Hall at All Souls. One of our valuable armorial teaspoons went missing. I wonder where it is now? and when it will turn up?

Veronica began very early with an immature biography of Strafford, for which I stood, a lay-figure, for some of Strafford's more intolerable characteristics. She inscribed my copy, 'Go thou, and do likewise!' I thought this a bit much from a young pupil to her tutor. I was in fact heavily engaged in research into Tudor Cornwall, but was getting too ill to bring it as yet to fruition. She later completely revised her book as *Thomas Wentworth*, in part owing to Cooper's unsparing criticisms.

She next justified herself by a large book on the vast subject of the Thirty Years War. As a Wedgwood, she was highly educated and knew the requisite languages. It was a remarkable achievement for a young scholar: G.N. Clark laid down that no one had accomplished a first-rate work of historical research under the age of thirty. She was not yet thirty, and the book was first-rate.

She next produced a brief biography of Oliver Cromwell, which again she revised years later. A translation, from German, of Brandi's large biography of the Emperor Charles V

111

followed. Then succeeded her own fine biography of William the Silent, a greater statesman than Elizabeth I, for where she ruled a nation ready-made for her, William of Orange had to create one – the Dutch, most brilliant of Europe's young nations.

The book won my sympathies for the heroic man. What he had to put up with from warring factions and factious individuals who would not pull together in a common cause! He was described one day sitting in the midst, head plunged in hands, while the disputes raged around him. Of course he couldn't keep the Netherlands united even against the enemy, Spain. They broke in two – the Catholic South, the Protestant North – Philip of Spain had William assassinated. England had to come to the rescue of the Dutch. (The Bismarckian Motley in his classic work disconsidered England's indispensable help in liberating Holland.)

Meanwhile Veronica was helping on the literary side to edit *Time and Tide*. This was Lady Rhondda's paper, from which John Betjeman was sacked for not being sufficiently 'global'. Lady Rhondda was global all right, both in her interests and her figure: one of those large spreading ladies described by Virginia Woolf as a 'lesbian of an old-fashioned sort'. Veronica, tactful as ever, was one of the few to get on with her and stay the course for some years. My old pupil called on me to write reviews. She herself was also translating – *Auto da Fe* by Elias Canetti. Privately she wrote novels to amuse herself, which were never published. She enjoyed a fixation on Prince Rupert – did she write a novel about him?

From Lady Rhondda she graduated to Jonathan Cape, where we kept in touch, for he was publishing my *Grenville* and *Tudor Cornwall*. Innocently I wrote to him that, if he would only publish this heavy work of research, I would one day write him a book that really would sell – and wrote *A Cornish Childhood* and *The Spirit of English History*. For my Series she was good enough to write *Richelieu and the French Monarchy*. I knew I could rely on my old pupil for a good book. We were good pals.

She began the busy 1950s with a book on Seventeenth Century

Literature. This draws attention to one of her chief qualities: we were both equally interested in literature and in history. For I continued to write poetry – which Eliot encouraged and published – in spite of the heavy drudgery of research. (My ill health eventually saved me from politics.) Veronica's combination of literature with history appeared again in a biography of Montrose, another of her heroes.

Then came her two big books on the Civil War, the summit of her work, *The King's Peace*, 1955, and *The King's War*, 1958. I much admired these works – which were less well received by pure academics of the John Cooper stripe. What was the quality that marked these volumes for me? She brought home the inextricable *confusion* of the struggle and the times.

How could the three kingdoms be possibly kept together? – One with an Anglican majority, another with a Presbyterian, a third with a Catholic? It was like the childhood game of getting three marbles into one, at most two, holes. Only the Crown could lock the three into some sort of acceptable system. With the Puritan attack on the monarchy, the failure of Charles I to keep control, the three kingdoms fell into inextricable confusion. Veronica rendered that as no one had done. Eventually some sort of unity was restored by force – the victory of the Puritans in England and their (Cromwell's) conquest of Scotland and Ireland.

She had intended a trilogy. Why then did she not go on to complete it? She told me that she lost interest. There was another explanation. The whole subject of the Civil War had become bogged down in academic controversy and hair-splitting, under the lead of dear, doctrinaire Christopher Hill.

But who *were* the Puritans? How to define them? Much doubt was expressed on this issue by the professors. Was there any such thing as a Presbyterian party? And who precisely were Independents? Etc. *ad nauseam*. It is true that when the lid was lifted off society all sorts of lunatics boiled up from below – Fifth Monarchy fanatics, Ranters, Soul-Sleepers, Muggletonians. Asses, of course – or, to vary the image, just like taking up a stone to see the insects pullulating beneath.

The controversies were so heated, the dons so rude to each

other – and dismissive of Veronica's work – that in my view she was not only put off, but frightened off. After all, she was not a don but a lady, of good manners, tactful and polite.

Then she surprised me. We were discussing the Civil War. I said how much I deplored the extremists on both sides who made it, and agreed with the sensible people in the middle – moderate Royalists like Falkland and Clarendon, moderate Parliamentarians like Selden, who were willing to compromise. Oh, no, said Veronica, she much preferred extremists, on both sides.

This shocked me. How could any rational person prefer the very people who were responsible for so much destruction and loss of life? I was also displeased at this, from a former pupil. It seemed to me that she was anxious to mark lines of difference of opinion. But was she justified on this issue?

There was a streak of doctrinairism in the Wedgwoods, which came out strongly in her uncle Josiah, the independent maverick MP, Colonel 'Josh', whose biography she was later to write. Not my type: I was not amused by him nor impressed by his capers. In her volume of essays, *Truth and Opinion*, I noticed other points of disagreement, our paths diverging. But I much appreciated her book, *The Trial of King Charles I*, which came out while I was in the USA, where it appeared as *A Coffin for King Charles*. Called upon to review it, I gave it a strongly favourable notice. Her sympathies here were all on the side of Charles I, hero of the tragedy. I have often had reason to notice how women's judgements in history are apt to be personal. One friend of ours wrote a book about the Princes in the Tower, in which she would have *liked* to find Richard III blameless, contrary to all the evidence, making every excuse for him. Other ladies have fallen for Sir Walter Ralegh – not realising that, though a man of genius, he was not a nice man. Elizabeth I and James I were right about him.

Two more books, *Poetry and Politics* and *Milton and his World* revealed again Veronica's admirable bringing together of literature and history. Here she and I were at one. These are cognate subjects that throw light on each other; the cross-fertilisation of these disciplines has fruitful results. The departmentalisation of studies can be sterilising and stultifying. Actually, historians are better read in literature than literary people are in history. Hence much of the fatuity of lit. crit. today. Without a knowledge of the Elizabethan age how can one properly understand Shakespeare, who so fully expressed it?

I remember once recommending a history class in the USA to read one of the finest of modern American poems, Robert Lowell's 'The Quaker Graveyard at Nantucket'. At that a not-so-bright young spark piped up. 'You should be in the English Literature department.' Ordinary minds never understand such things. Why bother them with them? Education is for the educable, not the uneducable. (Veronica would not allow me to say that in her blessed *Time and Tide*.)

She was a highly cultivated woman, with a real love of painting. She told me how to recognise a Crivelli. She thought of writing a biography of Vandyke, but gave up, thinking herself not qualified. She did however write a book on *The Political Career of Rubens*.

We were both at work in America, Veronica at the Princeton Institute, I at the Huntington Library. There I plodded away at Shakespeare's life and work, until I had worked out all the problems of the Sonnets – finding to my surprise that they all reduced to traditional common sense. It was not until I came back to Oxford that I discovered the identity of the Dark Lady in the Bodleian Library – just where she should be, and just *who* she would be: the musical young half-Italian discarded mistress of the Patron of Shakespeare's Company, Lord Chamberlain Hunsdon. How much nearer could you get? The discovery confirmed all my previous findings: I should never have got on to her if each one had not led me forward firmly, step by step.

Professor F.P. Wilson, head of the Eng. Lit. Faculty at Oxford, was the only person whom I told that the problems of the Sonnets had worked out consistently in every respect. His judgement of it – a cautious, conservative scholar – was: 'I am deeply impressed, and have nothing whatever to urge against it. If Hotson had told me I should know it was but another mare's nest.'

Coming back in the plane together from New York, I thought I would impart the secret to my old pupil. Oh, no – she would not hear of it! Her father, Sir Ralph, the railway magnate, had told her all about the Sonnets, she did not need to hear about them from me. I was astonished, and dismayed. Fancy not wanting even to go into the matter and check it with me! She would have found it all unanswerable, consistent in every bit by bit detail.

She compounded the offence later, when another of Hotson's mare's nests came out. On the mistaken assumption that Mr W.H. was Shakespeare's man in the Sonnets, instead of the publisher's man to whom they were dedicated, Hotson had 'discovered' that Shakespeare's young friend was William Hatcliffe, Prince of Purpoole in the Gray's Inn Revels. Dotty, of course. Hotson went further to 'discover' that Hilliard's miniature of an Unknown Young Man was a portrait of Shakespeare – totally unlike the authentic portrait we all know, the frontispiece to the First Folio. Hotson tended to spoil all his work by crazy conjectures.

Veronica was the only reputable scholar who gave him a favourable hearing, as if his rubbish might possibly be right!

This ended my friendship with her.

CHAPTER 18

Sir Lewis Namier

G.M. Trevelyan and L.B. Namier were at opposite poles as historians in my time. I do not think that they had much to say to each other, or even appreciated each other's work. As head of the profession and the most famous figure in the field Trevelyan may have even been nettled by the disproportionate cult that was made of Namier by the younger generation (my own), apt to discount the Master himself. He one day said to me, rather dismissively – and that was not like him – that Namier was 'a great researcher, but not a great historian'. He was probably bored with the *cult*, the fuss made about Namier.

For once that was not quite right. But it is very difficult to get Namier right – he was an extraordinary apparition on the English scene. We must try to do justice to both men – and the stark contrast between them may light up each.

We can see what Trevelyan meant. Namier had not written big synthetic works like the great historians, Gibbon or Macaulay, or Trevelyan himself. Namier's constructive book, which Pares thought his best, *England in the Age of the American Revolution*, remained a torso. It was specified as Volume 1, and Namier said that, if he went on with it, the next would be entitled 'The Rise of Parties'. For constitutional history this would have had greater significance, for it was the development of political parties and their organisation in Parliament that gradually eroded the powers of the Crown in government and took them over, to provide the executive.

Before this there had been his *Structure of Politics at the Accession of George III*, with its minute analysis of the

117

membership of the House of Commons in the Parliament of 1760–61, card-indexing them, breaking them down into the groups they formed and the affiliations they made. This book made a sensation. Namier got the credit of patenting a new method of minute analytical research, as if he had invented it. Historians raved about it, and followed his lead.

In fact he had got it from the famous card-index method of Sidney and Beatrice Webb, by whom Namier was much influenced on coming to England. G.N. Clark, who knew Namier well at Balliol, told me as much – people still do not realise the fact, though it appears clearly enough in his biography. Namier became a member of the Fabian Society, and later, in his maturity, came to favour 'the Welfare State, administered by Tories'. Not such a bad option, we may say – with its wise qualification.

He tells us that for forty years he had hoped to write his main work on Europe in the Nineteenth Century – a huge undertaking. From this he was distracted by various calls – war-work in the two German Wars,* for the Foreign Office, his Manchester professorship, and the devoted practical work he did in the noble cause of Zionism and saving what relics he could from the savagery of the Holocaust.

So in place of a large synthetic work we have half-a-dozen volumes of his essays and reviews, mainly on that period and our own. They all contain penetrating, sometimes prophetic insights – far superior to Macaulay's immature, complacent Essays, more profound and tragic in outlook in keeping with our time.

To point up the contrast. Trevelyan ranged over the whole of English history – with a foray into Italian – always from an English point of view. Namier was a European. He made a more original and much more influential onslaught on English eighteenth century history, with forays into the diplomatic

---

* Namier wrote, 'It were better if World War I and World War II were called the First and Second German Wars: which would define their origin and character, and their place in history.' I sometimes follow his usage which, however, betrays his European-centred viewpoint.

record; he then ranged over nineteenth century Europe and well into the twentieth, our own deplorable time.

Namier's mind was attuned to it, as Trevelyan's was to a better age. I was astonished once when Trevelyan let out that he disliked the world of post-Industrial Revolution. What? Not like the immense creativeness of the Victorian age – the summit of our history! In old age he regretted that he had not travelled more – he really knew only England and Italy. Namier knew Europe, and something of the United States.

He had a great advantage from his remarkable background. He was a Galician Jew, with a scholarly ancestry of cultivated standards. Exceptionally, his family were landowners, with small estates where he was brought up, not far from the Dniester, on the borders of Poland and Russia. They were cultured people, who knew languages and the civilised life of Vienna, Warsaw, Paris, Italy. His father was an admirer of John Stuart Mill. They were not practising Jews, but had an ecumenical attitude towards Catholic Christianity, while Namier himself had a curious admiration for the rigorous mind of Calvin.

There was an Old Testament strain in him. He *was* a judge, upright, with a conscience that never let him rest, a compassion for all down-trodden peoples. As an Eastern European he knew all about their sufferings, and spent much time helping refugees from German and Russian barbarism as well as his specific work for Israel. It was a marked compliment that he fell for English civilisation and institutions and made himself an authority on them.

He became a British citizen, and had something like a love-affair with our eighteenth century aristocracy. Something of an aristocrat himself, he had no sense of social inferiority, though full of complexes and resentments otherwise. At Balliol he was much of a favourite, if not a mascot; everybody recognised his brilliance.

He resented being turned down for a Fellowship at All Souls. I find that previously I have been wrong in thinking that there was no prejudice in the matter. A.F. Pollard, who was an examiner, wanted him elected; a majority did not. It was not so

119

much old-fashioned anti-Jewish prejudice as Namier's over-whelming personality. There was too much of him, he was an irrepressible bore; a very masculine type, he was quite imperceptive as to his effect on other people.

It was not only All Souls but Oxford that was at fault: the History Faculty would not have him as a professor. And this in spite of his lifelong loyalty to Balliol, and his tribute to Oxford as the place where he 'learned to think'. (I could say the same for myself.)

Thus we saw nothing of him in college, though Pares and I saw him at the Public Record Office. One evening after the day's work we were overtaken on the pavement in Kingsway by Uncle Lewis, who at once overwhelmed us with the misdeed of Sir John Fortescue in misdating a letter of George III in his edition of his letters. Namier devoted a volume to *Additions and Corrections* to only the first in poor Fortescue's edition. With that, I suspect, the publishers called a halt – a sense of proportion was wanting.

On another occasion he asked me out to tea. We went along to Twining's eighteenth century tea-house in Piccadilly, subse-quently destroyed by a German bomb. I settled for a chaste tea of Earl Grey and a cake. Not so Uncle Lewis: he ordered a double size chocolate ice-cream soda, topped up with cream. Having finished it, to my surprise he ordered a second – and at the end left me, his guest and much his junior, to pay for it. Neither of us was well off at the time, but I was amused by his imperceptiveness.

Oddly enough I have no memory of a subsequent occasion of which his widow gives an account in her biography of him.* It seems that our joint publishers, Macmillan, gave a lunch at the Dorchester for the publication of my book, *The Later Churchills*, when Namier gave the address. Why have I no memory of it?

* Julia Namier, *Lewis Namier. A Biography*, pp. 319–20.

Can it really have happened? I shall not be satisfied of it until I have time to go through my diaries for that decade.

Myself, I was not over-impressed by Namier's emphatic contribution to our knowledge of eighteenth century politics. It was not my period, and I thought it out of proportion. Pares was more devout and paid tribute to it. 'Books like Sir Lewis Namier's great work on *The Structure of Politics at the Accession of George III*, which have transformed our attitude to 18th century politics, have done so by virtue of a new outlook even more than by exploiting new manuscripts and exhibiting new detail.'

Was this book a 'great work', for all the fuss it made? Namier himself said that his chapters were really separate essays. It was not a constructive, organic whole, like Trevelyan's, or my own trilogy on the Elizabethan age.

This was however a seminal work; it not merely challenged but overthrew the dominant Whig interpretation of George III and his reign. This had come down from the party writings of Burke and the Foxite tradition incarnated in Sir George Otto Trevelyan's partisan work on the American Revolution.

George III was completely within his constitutional rights, in fact was a dedicated follower of the British Constitution. When the American colonies rebelled they were rebelling not against the Crown, but against the claims of Parliament to legislate for the whole Empire. This had been its constitutional right too, but the American colonies had outgrown it and claimed self-government. My old friend, Allan Nevins, thought that Dominion Status would have met the case. But the Revolution took place a hundred and fifty years before Dominion Status was invented, early this century. Thus, at the time, no solution was possible between the two absolute claims to 'rights', meaning really power.

Namier's whole tone was, as always, challenging. Like the great man he was, he never minded speaking out *in propria persona* for the benefit of those who did not know what, or how, to think. 'For political problems do not, as a rule, deeply affect the lives and consciousness of ordinary men, and little real thought is given to them by these men.'

The whole book illustrated and was a proof of this theme. It showed how little Party meant at the time – its effective development was subsequent. Men entered Parliament 'to make a figure', as Lord Chesterfield said – 'and no more dreamt of a seat in the House in order to benefit humanity than a child dreams of a birthday cake that others may eat it.' Namier was an enemy of political cant, particularly Whig cant, and some people didn't like his sharp exposure of it. True, Parliament provided the men to form government, but the sovereign was within his rights in appointing and constructing it. As for men's motives in wanting to make a figure in this representatively national assembly Pares later made a less trenchant gloss.

Namier would not sit for our Fellowship examination a second time, though advised to – and several Fellows have been elected on a second try. He kept touch however with T.E. Lawrence, whom he had known there. His sketches of him offer the most penetrating insight into that tortured personality. He recognised Lawrence's pursuit of pain, without labelling it precisely as masochism; also his strangling perverseness, without placing it among Lawrence's obvious Irish characteristics. In later life Namier became aware of his own perverseness and self-contradictions.

He had a much more incisive perception of character than Trevelyan had. This comes out in his portraits of George III, and Lord North, Metternich and the Princess Lieven, or Palmerston. He had a positive dislike of Burke and Whig cant. In this earlier half of his work he underestimated the importance of ideas – for which he was taken to task by my Cambridge friend, Professor Plumb. Later on he allowed them more place, perhaps more appropriately for the nineteenth century.

Interest in character went along with his pursuit of psychoanalysis, to which he subjected himself. He was psychotic, if not psychopathic, a much stranger character, with its inner tensions, than appeared in his formidable public persona. Though he was not brought up as a practising Jew, he

was a religious man addicted to prayer. In the end he was, like
T.S. Eliot, baptised as an Anglican. We must respect his
ecumenical attitude, longing for a reconciliation between
Judaism and Christianity.

It was a great compliment to Britain – in the last days of her
greatness and in the cruel tests of her struggle for existence –
that these two men of genius, Namier and T.S. Eliot, should
identify themselves with her – as Henry James did in the First
German War. It was easier for Eliot, of pure English descent, to
make himself over as an Englishman, even to his accent – which
so much irritated nasty Edmund Wilson. It was more difficult
for Namier who, though he wrote an excellent style, retained
always a foreign accent. The more one penetrates into his psyche
the stranger he becomes.

Among his gifts was a prodigious and exact memory, which
one sees at work in his devastating analyses of diplomatic
documents. He had Macaulay's gift of practically memorising a
page as a whole. His book *Diplomatic Prelude 1938–9* greatly
impressed me, for – before even the documents were published –
he had forecast the course of negotiations.

He had an epigrammatic wit, but little sense of humour. (Who
had among historians? Gibbon and, curiously enough, the
pompous Clarendon; Macaulay, even the grouchy Carlyle;
Maitland, for all the inaptness of his subject.) When Ramsay
MacDonald deserted the Labour Party in 1931, Godfrey Elton
followed him, and was made, a peer. He had been the tutor of
MacDonald's son at Oxford, whom his father made an
Under-Secretary. Namier floated the dictum: 'In my period
peers made their tutors under-secretaries; today Under-
Secretaries make their tutors peers.'

We had much more to learn from the other half of Namier's
work, his writings on European history, especially Central and
Eastern Europe, Austria–Hungary and Germany. Here he was
on home ground and knew the score intimately, as the British
and Anglo-Saxons generally did not.

During the 1914–18 War he had worked in and for the Foreign Office. He knew well how ignorant the outcry against the Versailles settlement was, and how stupid the Revisionists were, playing into Germany's hands. The territorial provisions were on the whole fair, rectifying great wrongs. They liberated the Baltic states, the Slavs of southern Europe, and recreated Poland. In fact Lloyd George pushed through a change of the Polish Corridor's frontier in favour of the Germans in a minority there, which was unfair to the Polish majority.

I remember Lloyd George defending the settlement, at the Oxford Union, against a doctrinaire Liberal, one Pringle, who could not see a 'scintilla' of justice in the Versailles Treaty. The real grievance of the Germans was simply that they had lost their war. Namier was exceptionally well informed about all this, and the run-up to 1914. In a devastating analysis of the Imperiod Chancellor Bülow's Memoirs, he writes, 'Were any justification required for Great Britain's attitude to Germany during those years none better could be found than in this volume. The exotic schemings of the Emperor, his offer of the old Kingdom of Burgundy to the King of the Belgians; his plan to force Denmark into a political surrender to Germany; the German calculations how much longer they would have to mind their conduct towards Great Britain, i.e. how soon their fleet would enable them to assume a different tone; and finally, the prospect of such an instrument in the hands of a man whom Bülow himself describes as irresponsible and downright psychopathic – who, in view of these facts frankly admitted by the ex-Chancellor, can say that either our suspicions or our caution were unfounded?'*

Such indeed was the pre-1914 Germany which Britain had to confront.

In 1914 German deliberately unleashed the war by backing Austria–Hungary's attack on Serbia. Chancellor Bethmann–Holweg blurted out that they would never have a better excuse for making it. The American guru George Kennan has expressed regret for the disappearance of Austria–Hungary – as if it were

* L.B. Namier, *In the Margin of History*, p. 225.

ever possible to put that Humpty-Dumpty together again! Born and brought up an Austro–Hungarian subject Namier knew better than that out-of-date, nineteenth century view. The ethnic minorities, rival nationalities, were all determined to have their own way and set up their own states – we see them at it again today. Between the wars Czechoslovakia was the most successful of these succession states; today even Czechs and Slovaks cannot live together – let alone the rest!

At one point Namier drops the word 'lunacy' into the melting pot: one sympathises – human affairs are very silly. The leading English authority on these peoples in the inter-years, Seton-Watson, concluded that they were 'all mad, and could not see beyond the end of their nose.' *Verb. sap.* Namier's essay, 'The Downfall of the Habsburg Monarchy', gives us a definitive survey of all this mess.*

Namier understood that there *is* such a thing as national character – he has several penetrating essays on the subject – as evidenced in history. In a nation the collectivity adds up to something more than the sum of the individuals. One may love France and appreciate the French; but the French collectivity is selfish, self-interested and short-sighted (witness 1940), ego-tistic and rhetorical (witness Louis XIV, Napoleon, de Gaulle). There is something light-headed and operatic about the Italians, *opéra bouffe* with Mussolini, as the English thought.

The English collectively are slack and easy-going, they forget easily – they forgot what they suffered at the hands of the Germans in the years 1914–18. And their upper classes suffer from a superiority complex, which makes for complacency. They were all complacent about Hitler and the Nazis until too late – one used to hear them pooh-poohing Hitler in the 1930s. Though Chamberlain's Foreign Secretary, Halifax, never bothered to read *Mein Kampf*, in which the programme was made clear for all to read.

* Reprinted in his *Vanished Supremacies*.

Namier knew too well what the German collectivity added up to – the vast mass occupying the strategic centre of Europe – overbearing and bullying at best (Bismarck), with an inflamed inferiority complex, far more dangerous than a complacent superiority complex, a combination of sentimentality about themselves with brutality towards others. Still, no one could have dreamed what they were capable of when they got on top ...

Namier did his best to warn against the complacent, and ignorant, course of Appeasement. We do not need to go into any more here. The upshot was all too clear. Cadogan, whom Chamberlain pushed in to take Vansittart's place in the Foreign Office, admitted, 'It has all worked out as Van said it would – *and I never believed it.*'

Though I saw little of Namier in the dreadful 1930s – he never came to All Souls – I kept in sketchy contact. I saw eye to eye with him over the way things were going. We both kept on with our uphill campaign against Chamberlain's infatuated course – in vain.

In a valedictory essay, 'The German Finale to an Epoch in History', Namier sums up: 'Hitler and the Third Reich were the gruesome and incongruous consummation of an age which, as none other, believed in progress and felt assured that it was being achieved. The 150 years 1789–1939 were an era of confident hope and strenuous endeavour, of trust in the human mind and in the power of reason.'*

What an awakening we had! – at least those of us who did awake ...

To return to my theme. This points up the contrast with Trevelyan – whose eyes were set on Italy, sick enough with Mussolini, but who was more of a Little Englander, bemused by Baldwin. Namier had a more powerful intellect, more probing and incisive, while Trevelyan was the more dedicated artist. Trevelyan *concentrated* on his writing; though he did his full duty as citizen and public figure, he did not allow that to deflect him – hence his monumental achievement.

* *Vanished Supremacies*, p. 176.

18. Sir Lewis Namier

Namier had many distractions, in his private life as in public affairs, from the tragic epoch he lived through. All the same, what a compliment his work is to the nation he adopted, and what reason we have to be proud of him!

CHAPTER 19

A.J.P. Taylor

Taylor was the most controversial, and controverted, of all our historians. It is almost impossible to strike a balance about him, and he himself made it difficult even to be fair to him. I knew him from the time he was an undergraduate and was familiar with his mixed-up private life – trapped between two wives, each with a family, with a third, a Continental love-match, waiting in the wings. Oh, how complicated! He appears as a victim – no credit to his judgement; but it *is* to his credit that he carried on and got through so much work amid constant strains and stresses.

His private life is no concern of ours here – except for this consideration, that the mix-up eventually carried over into his work. He was a brilliant journalist – with the vocational disease of journalism: that it has to catch the moment and the attention at all costs, often at the cost of truth or conscience, or any sense of responsibility. He tells us that he didn't take himself seriously.

He was a gifted lecturer, who could hold any audience captive with his talks – he tells us that he made them up as he went along. He was a star performer on television, and always played to the gallery, for a laugh, a dismissive remark that appealed, or an epigram that was often a half-truth and still more often superficial or wrong-headed. He didn't seem to care – and that was unfair to himself, betrayed his own undoubted gifts.

What were these?

Liveliness, zest, originality, incisiveness – if all over the place, strokes all round the wicket – independence of mind. What was wanting was something essential to a good historian –

judgement, integrity. The word never appears in his work, and I don't think it meant anything to him. Nor do I think his work earned the respect of such men as Trevelyan, a crucial test – which consoles me in the unfavourable opinion I have of his work.

I must confess why. Taylor was a man of the extreme Left, but as such he lent himself to Beaverbrook's irresponsible attacks on the responsible leadership of the Labour Party, especially Ernest Bevin, against the United Nations, along with his rooted anti-Americanism. Taylor says that Beaverbrook bribed him, 'as he bribed everybody', particularly that group of irresponsible *Tribune* Leftists, Michael Foot, Tom Driberg, Muggeridge.

Though I am not very shockable, this line of theirs shocked me. I detest political irresponsibility, it does so much damage. It is particularly reprehensible in an historian, who bears a responsibility to the public, for his judgements and his absolute duty to state the truth, without fear or favour.

Taylor's judgements were all over the place. Fancy describing Beaverbrook as a 'great historian', when he knew very well that Beaverbrook invented episodes that never took place, falsified the evidence! Fancy a Leftist Socialist paying public tribute to Sir Oswald Mosley, the anti-Semitic Fascist leader, as the most original political thinker of the time! – and taking meals off him at the Ritz.

Were his judgements of fellow historians any better?

He described E.H. Carr as 'without rival among contemporary historians. His *History of Soviet Russia* is a masterpiece of scholarship and narration.' It is well known that E.H. Carr was completely taken in by Soviet propaganda, and reproduced in his books as reliable all their fake statistics. Carr also wrote a book advocating Appeasing Hitler as 'political realism', regardless of the consequences!

We come to a really great historian with Jakob Burckhardt, the most seminal and original historian of the nineteenth century. All recognise his great book, *The Civilisation of the Renaissance in Italy*, as an enduring masterpiece, for it still stands out today as a living influence, when most works of his time are forgotten. Not so Taylor. For him Burckhardt 'carries a handicap in the shape of this book. This handicap has been overcome. Henceforth we shall be taught to admire him for what he did not put down on paper, not for what he did.'

I regard this as disgraceful. His judgements of fellow Leftists are no better. E.P. Thompson wrote a History of the Working Class, regarded as a classic by his fellows. Not so by Taylor: 'I see no signs of brains at all.' Something the poor fellow had written was 'sheer gibberish'. Taylor had no high opinion of his fellow traveller with Beaverbrook, Michael Foot: 'one day his Menshevik charms will be exhausted'.

Taylor gives a devastating account of his old friend, Malcolm Muggeridge, whom I met with him in earlier days at Oxford. Muggeridge was never my man, but he was at least right about the nature of Communist rule in Russia. Taylor would not accept this: he remained consistently pro-Communist Russia, whatever his frequent inconsistencies and contradictions of himself.

His judgements of historical figures are equally unreliable. Fancy summing up Wellington as a 'silly old goose, constantly expecting the social roof to fall in'. Well, the roof had fallen in, with the French Revolution. Anyone who lived through that epoch, and had to cope with its consequences, knew how fragile the crust of civilisation is, and how fearful the consequences to a society of falling through. The proper appreciation of an historical figure is to go by the evidence, not personal prejudice. Appreciation of Wellington is a touchstone of good judgement. To know what this remarkable man was really like, read Stanhope's *Conversations* with him.

Alan one day said to me, 'When you say a "great man", you only mean that he is quicker on the trigger.' I dislike this kind of cheap cynicism – shocking in an historian. I said, 'Look, I have no prejudice in favour of Oliver Cromwell. But consider: one, when the Civil War began he was but a civilian, in the course of it he proved himself about the ablest commander in the field. Two, when at the end of it things were breaking apart, he grappled with the situation and held the three kingdoms together in his grip. He was surely a great man.'

That shut Alan up. There should have been more people to tell him to stop talking (and writing) nonsense. However, he would not take telling from anybody, least of all from me, whom he once called his 'oldest friend'. I did not regard him as a friend, we were not on the same wavelength.

The impersonal point here is that these snap judgements, snapping like a rat-trap, were utterly characteristic. He did not stop to consider. This was what made his lectures and television performances so popular, for popular audiences are incapable of judging – all the more reason to be responsible with them. As Vice-Chancellor Wheare said to me, 'That sort of cynicism goes a long way with undergraduates.'

No wonder the History Faculty at Oxford never wanted him for a professor. Oddly enough, he never understood that, or why.

He did not begin with any thought of becoming an historian, that happened almost accidentally. His writing career began with diplomatic history, as a protégé of Namier at Manchester. He graduated respectably with books in this field, particularly in regard to Central Europe. The drawback to diplomatic history is that it is apt to be one-track, one-dimensional, omitting in part the political background, and still more the social and economic factors conditioning it.

C.A. Macartney at All Souls, whose field this was, particularly Central Europe where he had lived, regarded Taylor's view of it as unsound. But, then, he was pro-Hungarian, where Alan was pro-Slav. He himself regarded his summary, *The Struggle for Mastery in Europe*, as his 'dullest' book, so perhaps it was more reliable. His favourite was the *Trouble-makers* about British foreign policy in the nineteenth century. They had all his sympathy, for he was a trouble-maker himself; they may have been sometimes right – over the Crimean War, for example.

I recommended his brief *Course of German History* as useful at the time, though scored here and there by those dreadful snap judgements. Luther objected to the sale of indulgences to benefit Rome, 'if it had been for the purpose of massacring German peasants, Luther might never have become a Protestant.' Quite untrue; however displeasing Luther was, one must be fair. All my sympathies are, of course, with Erasmus, who stood for civilised values.

I suggested Bismarck as a subject to Alan for my Series. He took it, more lucratively, and understandably, to his own publisher. His estimate of Bismarck was too favourable, to my liking: he let him off the hook, as he was to do, very largely, Hitler later on. The American Professor Cole, in his survey of Taylor's work, thinks that he was taken with Bismarck's forceful, bullying personality. More important, he omitted to notice that Bismarck destroyed the chances of representative Parliamentary government growing up in his Germany – he called it 'the Revolution', and achieved the unification of Germany by 'blood and iron', in his words. The consequence was to put back Europe by a century, and ultimate disaster for Germany itself – though Germans couldn't see it.

Here I may cite the fact that Adenauer, West Germany's Chancellor after the Second War, had no illusions about Bismarck – he knew too well what it had led to, both for Germany and Europe.

My reservations about Taylor as historian were increasing, but I was affronted by his account of *The Origins of the Second World War*. (Isaiah Berlin commented, it was 'spitting on Namier's grave'.) It was utterly irresponsible to argue that Hitler was not much more responsible for the Second War than we were. He may have been a criminal, but other politicians were not much better, etc. This time I was not only shocked, but angry. I knew the way that pro-Nazis would use it as excuse: four such sympathisers in Germany came out in their papers with 'Germany not responsible for the War: Oxford Professor Says So.'

Anybody who has read *Mein Kampf* knows that Hitler meant war – war with Russia, and after victory the rest would follow: the domination of Europe. We should be at his mercy. Naturally he would not want a superfluous war with Britain, if she were prepared to give way, as he appears to have expected – a second Munich.

What people were not intelligent enough to realise – except in the Foreign Office – was the following. Hitler was *Plan-mässig*: he had a plan worked out in his mind, nobody more so, but as a politician he was pragmatic enough to allow for contingencies, take advantage of opportunities, even change course for a time, as with the Russo-German Pact.

This is a simple intellectual point: taking one's opportunities does not prevent one from having a long-term plan. Taylor, having no judgement, had made the same mistake over Bismarck as he now made over Hitler.

Further, what the readers of the book were not intelligent enough to notice was that, in letting Hitler off, Taylor was making the German people responsible. In fact the German people did not welcome their Second War, as they had done the First. But they had let themselves in for Hitler and the Nazis; Hindenburg, their hero of the First War, had put them in power, and the German objectives of the Second War were continuous with those of the First.

The books of the leading German authority on this, Fritz Fischer, make this perfectly clear. Taylor seems to have learned nothing from him: he was not out to learn anything from anybody, he always had his own views. From the first I foresaw the damage Taylor's book would do; I protested in letters to the *Times Literary Supplement*. That book ended any friendship with him. Again he never understood why. There are still third-rate brains about who are mixed up about these issues – but not, I fancy, in the Foreign Office.

Alan actually thought himself qualified to be the official editor of our Foreign Office Documents between the wars! Once more nobody else thought so, but he made a continual fuss about their editing in the *Times Literary Supplement*. E.L. Woodward and R.D'O. Butler, of All Souls, responsible people, were made official editors. They were sniped at by Alan from time to time, but didn't bother to reply – they had taken his measure.

Then came the question of the Regius Professorship at Oxford. There would have been no question if Richard Pares had not been mortally stricken: he would have been the obvious choice. As it was, the chair went begging. Lucy Sutherland turned it down. Trevelyan wanted me. I couldn't possibly have done the job, with my health record; anyway, I wanted only to write, be independent and free to go to America half the year, winters in California at the Huntington Library. With Trevelyan I gave my support to Trevor-Roper as a *pis-aller*, though young for the job.

Taylor seems to have expected it. I was horrified at the idea of the author of *The Origins of the Second World War* becoming our official spokesman. Trevor-Roper was right on that crucial issue. Alan never forgave Namier for not backing him sufficiently strongly. But the Regius Professorship was not in his gift, and he may have had reservations. From that moment Taylor broke off all relations with his old patron, and would not even send a message to him on his death-bed. Surely there was something psychologically unstable there.

The simple fact was that the Faculty did not want Alan as a professor. Need one wonder? A leading figure in the School calls him 'a dishonest historian'. I never went so far: it was the *irresponsibility* that discredited him for me. This worthy twice backed Taylor for a chair! God, where are *standards* today?

Who was to write the final volume in the Oxford History of England? As we have seen, G.N. Clark thought of doing it himself, but decided to offer it to Taylor, since there was no one obvious about. R.C.K. Ensor wrote the preceding volume, one of the best. His view of a course of BBC lectures by Alan was, 'The substance consisted too largely of shallow half-truths, more dangerous than plain untruths, because more specious, yet not a bit more trustworthy.'

That may serve for a serious historian's view of Taylor's work. Clark's editorship may have made a difference, for there emerged from it the best of Taylor's books, *English History, 1870–1945*. One can admire the spread of the book, the skilled control he kept on the mass of information, the sheer sprawl of the period, the amount of work he put into it, and yet the zest with which he kept it all alive. Clark may have pruned some of the usual *boutades*: plenty were left.

One may give him credit for not having been an Appeaser, and also for his plumping for Lloyd George as the dynamic leader of the nation in the First War. He need not have been so contemptuous of Asquith. It is noticeable that H.A.L. Fisher, though an ardent admirer of Lloyd George, yet had a just appreciation of Asquith.

Why then did I not like the book?

I did not like its populist stance, his constant pose as the people's man, their Honest John. His background was middle class, Manchester money (quite a lot of it: his grandfather was worth half-a-million.) All that Leftist group, Crossman (Double Crossman, Bowra called him), the Foots, Driberg, Muggeridge, George Orwell, Kingsley Martin, who gave them the lead in forever attacking Ernest Bevin ("'ow long before you'll be stabbin' us in the back?') – they were all middle class. I did not need their illusions about the working class, any more than Ernest Bevin did.

Alan had accepted this job with alacrity, he thought of it as a kind of rehabilitation. Henceforth G.N. Clark got good reviews from that all too ready pen.

When Beaverbrook died it fell to Alan to write the official biography. This was a labour of love, for he declared at the beginning, 'I loved the man.' This meant that there was no critical judgement of this controversial character, who had an appalling record about Appeasement, telling the public in 1939, what they wanted to hear: 'There will be no war this year.' When Michael Foot & Co. wrote their indictment of the Appeasers, *Guilty Men*, they entirely omitted the name of one of the foremost of them, their patron, Beaverbrook. We may fairly say that hypocrisy was the vocational disease of that indefensible group.

Though Alan knew the man all too well, he did not penetrate to the clue to his personality. Beaverbrook put himself across as a son of the manse. His father was a quiet, sober Scotch-Canadian Presbyterian minister. But his mother was Irish, and Beaverbrook's character was recognisably Irish: warm and generous to those whom he took to, nasty and vindictive to those who crossed his path, given to feuds and vendettas.

Alan profited immensely from this relationship – starred in

Beaverbrook's papers, constantly entertained at Cherkley, all the cheeses and claret. In return Beaverbrook's unreliable books were reviewed as masterly. His papers, with Lloyd George's, constituted a library, of which Alan was made librarian, with its perks – editing the Diary of Frances Stevenson, Lloyd George's mistress, later wife. Meanwhile the fat biography was a best-seller. (Actually, I had been asked, by both sides of the Lloyd George family, to write the official biography of the great man. Fortunately I was saved – for the Elizabethan age and Shakespeare – by the advice of my trusted friend, Professor Jack Simmons.)

Taylor did well out of all this. So that it comes as a surprise that, after it was all over, he wrote that Beaverbrook 'was not worth it. I wasted my time with him.' How can one respect such weathercock judgements? They point to psychological instability. And they wreck respect for his work as an historian. It was a thousand pities, for he had remarkable gifts. It must be said of him that he was his own worst enemy; on the other hand, he could not help himself.

Some of his gifts were concealed. He had a passionate love of music; he loved church architecture and landscape. None of this appeared in the rather bleak texture of his work, his snappy, epigrammatic style. So that I thought of him, mistakenly, as a Philistine.

All the time he was struggling with family worries, the pressures and strains of notoriety, controversy, popularity. Was he perhaps stimulated, energised by this? Graham Greene confessed to a mistress that he could not write unless he was inspired by – what he regarded as – living in sin. Alan had no such religious belief, but was it possible that he was a comparable psychological case?

CHAPTER 20

Richard Pares

By Richard Pares's death in his early fifties the study of eighteenth century England and her colonies suffered its most grievous loss. He was a parallel to Namier, whom he admired without being a disciple. As an Englishman he had a subtler sense of English society – no love-affair with it – and he had a better sense of proportion. His interest in the subject was as much economic as political. He did not share Namier's excruciating concentration on political minutiae; indeed he had a severe idea of politics, 'the world of the second-best'. Historians concentrate too much on politics, as the newspapers do. Culture, literature, the arts are more rewarding, and writers more interesting than politicians. Not but what Richard – my dearest friend at All Souls – was a most cultured man, a very well-read Wykehamist, with a particular love of Jane Austen.

There was a paradox about him. He was, with David Cecil, the most brilliant and amusing conversationist I have known. He did not allow this to appear in his writing. He began with an inhibited (and inhibiting) view of history and what historical writing should be.

It was curious to me that he should have had no hunch, no inspiration as to the field of work or subject he should embark on. When jostled into the eighteenth century, on which he spent his life, he seemed to have no affection, hardly any liking, for it. Whereas I loved the subjects that came naturally my way – Cornwall, the Tudors (Celts mostly), the Elizabethan age, Shakespeare.

Richard had taken Greats at Balliol, and thought first of taking up the Roman Principate. Then he fancied a career in journalism, and tried the *Liverpool Post*. Saved from that fate, he came back to Oxford, where Kenneth Bell said, 'What about Sugar?' Sugar it was. Though I thought that odd, it led him into the history of eighteenth century trade, the colonies, economic imperialism, and of course politics. As he wrote later, when he came to grips with it: 'The most important thing in the history of an empire is the history of the mother country.' Australians might note that – their finest historian, Keith Hancock, understood it well.

Talk about grip! Pares threw himself upon the subject, like committing rape; or, a more proper image, he shut himself up in it like entering a convent. It became his vocation. He exhausted the materials relevant to it in Oxford and London, then set off for the archives in the USA and in the West Indies. In the climate of Jamaica and Barbados, he told me, he was sometimes turning over papers that mouldered into dust as he finished with them.

After some years of inhuman concentration he emerged with a mountain of a manuscript of over three hundred thousand words. It was not a book, and it was not publishable. G.N. Clark and Namier wrestled with it, and excavated a big important book, *War and Trade in the West Indies, 1739–1763*, a by-product, *Colonial Blockade and Neutral Rights*, over the same period, and two weighty articles for the *English Historical Review*. Lucy Sutherland, from a position to know, described the heavy main volume as 'an authoritative work of many-sided learning and confident judgement, though it suffers from a young scholar's desire to do too many things at once.'

It is indeed opaque, a wood difficult to penetrate for the trees. It was hard to take in until I came to a portrait sketch of the first Trelawny Governor of Jamaica. The moment my interest was aroused it was switched off. I asked Richard why he had not gone on with it. 'Oh,' he said dismissively, 'I didn't think that was history.' It was mere biography, and that – as against Carlyle, and so many others – was not history. I did not agree, but did not answer back: he was the professional.

When I brought out *Sir Richard Grenville of the 'Revenge'*, he was not best pleased. True, it was a by-product of my researches into Tudor Cornwall, in which I was buried for years. But I should never have been able to shape up that portrait of a society later, had I not had the experience of writing a biography first – chronology, construction given. Moreover, Grenville was a significant gap among Elizabethans, asking to be filled. There were even technical difficulties about the subject to surmount, if Richard had wanted to know. (I owed my introduction into the Public Record Office, prison-like building, to him. He showed me the ways of it, and we worked – or overworked – both of us there together.)

We did not impinge upon each other's work – he was a great one for non-impinging, essentially reticent, and 'impinge' was a frequent term of derogation with him. Perhaps I was apt to impinge, with my political interests and associations in the Labour Party, and there I carried him along with me. He was a loyal friend and associate there – with G.D.H. Cole, and his revivified Fabian group, the Society for Socialist Inquiry and Propaganda, backed by Ernest Bevin, for what good it was.

If one were to compare Pares with McFarlane – they did not make much of each other – both were professionals. And both were inhibited and repressed in their view of history (both, significantly, from unhappy family backgrounds). Richard had a brilliant, toublesome father, Sir Bernard Pares, whom he reacted against. Sir Bernard was married to Russia, rather than his family: he was obsessed with Russia, a bore about it. But he was a gifted lecturer, a star platform performer around the country, very well known in his day.

His father's popular appeal, his personal magnetism, his very readable books – that was what Richard meant by what was 'not history'. His family experience had made him a sadly *désabusé* man. He was not only a no-nonsense man, but had a real touch of cynicism about human beings, a sensitive nose for cant and humbug. Perhaps this was not out of place for his subject – eighteenth century politicians gave plenty of scope for it – and he would cite Charles II's remark about some successful politician's 'nonsense suiting their nonsense'. Part of the paradox was that Richard was such a scintillating person himself, so amusing a talker, an enchanting man, the opposite

139

pole to the dry-as-dust he would have imposed on us. He
changed as he grew older.

He had the advantage of Greats, the classical background, and
wide reading. He was a cleverer man, a more nimble mind than
McFarlane, well able to hold his own with David Cecil and
Isaiah Berlin. He had no use for philosophy, and despised
metaphysical palaver. (So did Wittgenstein.) I recall Tony
Quinton, much amused by this, asking what he would have in
place of it. Richard replied without hesitation, 'More history!'

Then too Pares had a wider conspectus. His concern with
economic affairs and trade led him to consider economic
imperialism – he read Marx and the arguments of Rosa
Luxemburg – and this tied in with the problems of colonialism.
His intellectual honesty told him that it was absurd – in fact
popular humbug – to say that the balance was all to the bad.
Colonies profited, were enriched, by it as well as the mother
country. He knew the facts, and did not trade in slogans. He
acknowledged the evil that was in the scale – 'think of the slave
trade in the past and the colour bar in the present [now vanished
too] – though we may hope that it is outweighed by an even
larger heap of good.' 'On the whole, as things are, our
interference brought about more good than evil.' In my own view
it is self-evident that that was true of that most exceptional
record in history, British rule in India. (We must remember that
it was an Anglo-Indian empire, run by the co-operation of the
Indians.)

Consider, if 'we did little until lately for the social welfare of
these peoples, we were not doing much more even for the social
welfare of our own people. But would they have done more for
themselves at that time?' The answer is evidently – not. Writing
in the 1950s, he said, 'It has yet to be proved that nationalism
will, in the long run, do the world less harm than imperialism.'
How about that for an historian's foresight? Look round at the
world today!

As for the historical record, contrary to popular slogans (even
graffiti scribbled by immigrants on our walls), 'colonial powers
derived only a very small part of their capital from their
dealings with their colonies. In fact they were building up the

capital of their colonies even faster than their own.' In the course of history how many imperial powers have been willing to hand over for dependencies to govern themselves? He knew no earlier example than that of Britain. In the eighteenth century everybody (including George III) thought that the loss of the American colonies would be the end of Britain as a power. Since Pares wrote, France has handed over in Algeria. Can we say that Algeria is any the happier for it? Or, for that matter, Vietnam?

With his knowledge of the Roman *imperium* Pares saw that the Romans exacted tribute from their subject peoples – as in Britain, where Seneca, the moralist, profited from investment there. Why not? – In return for internal peace, stability and security. In my view, Cogidubnus, the sub-Roman king of the region around Chichester, did better for his people by co-operating with Roman rule than by confrontation with the legions. It was a more intelligent policy, and it paid dividends.

In studying the pros and cons of Colonialism Pares had the advantage of his exploration of business history, a new genre which he virtually patented. In 1950 he produced an admirable book, *A West India Fortune*, based on the papers of the Pinneys, a merchant family operating from Bristol. In giving it to me he said, 'Here, Professor, is a book of which, I think, you will approve.' 'Why?' 'Because it has a beginning, a middle, and an end.' So he had learned that lesson at last. That was what I held that a book should be – an organic whole.

He always called me 'Professor', I suppose because I wasn't one. And when he learned that I never wished to be, he declared that now his 'withers were wrung'. It was natural, with his professorial background, that his horizons should have been academic. (And he made a dynastic marriage, to Professor Powicke's daughter.) For a decade or so he held a chair at Edinburgh, and 'enjoyed every minute of it'. What impressed me more was the astonishingly judicious paper he wrote, 'A Quarter of a Millennium of Anglo-Scottish Union'.

Here again was that characteristic concern of those

middle-class writers – Clark, McFarlane, Pares – with how
things worked. Not my line: I was more interested by how things
were, and in particular, how they *looked*.

Pares planned a parallel book on a London West India
merchant house. Before the Second German War engulfed us,
and destroyed so much, 'the partners of the house kindly allowed
me to spend a whole winter and spring working through their
oldest archives.' He had got through the first thirty years of this
house's history before the blow fell – 'the Germans came and the
beautiful office with the counter, the carved fireplace and –
worst of all – the archives, went up in flames.' This took place in
the great air-raid of 29 December 1940, a minute portion of the
destruction wrought upon the City – and its history. By then
Richard was hard at work, appropriately, as a wartime civil
servant in the Board of Trade.

He made a first-class civil servant by all accounts. Of course
he overworked (as H.W.C. Davis had done in the first of our two
German Wars – both died in their early fifties). Richard worked
all day at his war effort, and all evening and half the night
editing the *English Historical Review*. It was an inhuman
strain.

For his distinctive contribution to the war effort in the Board
of Trade Pares had served a kind of apprenticeship by his
eighteenth century researches. Problems of trade, the Navy and
naval policy, its manning, blockade, conflicts with neutrals,
neutral rights – he had studied and written about all these
matters. His professorship ended with the onset of multiple
sclerosis, which eventually killed him. He came back to All
Souls, to which we both owed so much. Indeed he said that it was
'the library, traditions, and conversation of All Souls which had
formed his mind as a historian.' (Oddly enough, that may have
been more true for him than for me: it turned my mind towards
politics. But that too had its advantages for an historian.)

Since Richard could no longer dwell in the archives, his mind
turned more – and advantageously – to general history. He
reflected on it much more than usual with historians, for he had

a clever working brain. 'Historians, in asking why and why not, are seeking for a coherent system of explanations, and above all of causation, for history is especially a study of causality.' For all the differences between individuals, we recognise the uniformity of human nature. Historians are engaged in 'the construction of that intermediate kind of sense which is the most that they can safely try to make of history.'

It was a very restrictive view. Paradoxically it suppressed Pares's own exceptional brilliance, to confine him (and us) to the dry-as-dust and routine. Characteristically he did not like a brilliant man, a man of genius like Chatham, he preferred the 'dear Duke', Newcastle, whom at one point he calls the 'silly old fool'. Newcastle was a comic figure in his time and is a figure of fun all through Horace Walpole's Letters. I do not think he was such a fool as they made out. True, he had 'weak nerves' and was apt to cry at opposition, but to have held on to power for some twenty years, in that world of faction, shows inner toughness and some ability. Moreover, when people emphasise aristocratic corruption, note that Newcastle *spent* his large fortune on politics, and made nothing out of it. He must have been concerned for the interest of the country, if also, quite naturally, of his class.

Richard and I did not see eye to eye about all this. I admired the man of genius – however intolerable, Chatham; we argued about him and all that. In the end Richard admitted that he was the greatest war minister the country ever had (a remote kinsman of Churchill's), and went so far as to describe him as the only living human being in a show of shadows. Of course large stretches of history are dreary, but also there is drama, excitement, brilliance; heroism, self-sacrifice, tragedy; pathos, even poetry. There was much of that in Richard's own life – a matchless example of courage, fortitude, stoicism – but he would not transfer that to history.

He also was in favour of the professionals' habit of putting up some thesis or other, which was then challenged by other professionals, and there ensued a controversy. As over the Crisis of the Seventeenth Century, or the Rise of the Gentry. He thought that out of the clash of opinions the truth emerged. I questioned this. For one thing, people dug their heels in and stuck to their previous opinions. Why not stick to facts and confront the issue simply, in and for itself? I wasted no time on the controversy, though it raged all over my field: all the facts showed that the Gentry rose. Similarly with the Elizabethan age, the background of Shakespeare's life and work, I do not waste time on controversy with people who are not qualified by an intimate knowledge of the facts: these are irrefutable and in time will prevail. As for 'the Crisis of the Seventeenth Century' – *every* century has witnessed crisis: what about the sixteenth century, or the fifteenth, or indeed our own?

'No questions, no history,' wrote Pares: thesis, antithesis, synthesis. This was not for me – too Hegelian; I was not persuaded of this in Marx – too rigid and categorical for the subtlety, the confusion, the *flow* of history. Moreover, in a throwaway phrase, Richard answered himself. 'All historians are imposing, all the time, a pattern of their own discovery upon their material – *except pure narrators*.' I italicise that qualifying clause, for it gives the argument to narrative history, truer to the facts of what actually happened, without the intervention of professionals' theses about them. 'A fig for Opinion!' says William Shakespeare, the historian.

Of course we agreed about a great deal, though Richard hardly allowed for an element, even a scintilla, of idealism any more than Namier did. Yet there must be *some* element of idealism somewhere for a society to hold together, even if interest is overwhelmingly more important. He was disgusted, worn down, by cant, particularly by the political cant of the Whigs and Tories in his period, 'which illustrates the general uselessness of these superannuated labels'. Look at the silly 'shibboleths' that kept Chatham's and Rockingham's factions fatally apart, when they were really at one about the crucial question of the American colonies.

We were of a mind that historians were apt 'to write the wrong kind of books, about the wrong kind of subject'. Who wants any more books about the Great Wardrobe, or the Chamber, under Edward II, or indeed the chamber in the Wardrobe? Or any more biographies of popular subjects, Mary Queen of Scots or

Elizabeth I, Charles I or Oliver Cromwell, when there are so many lesser figures we want to know about? What about family history? – when families are often the effective units in social history. Or local, regional history, when localities, regions have a character of their own, and make a distinctive contribution to general history, or that of people, nation, continent?

How perceptive, how superior to the general run, Pares was when at last he condescended to biography! He was just about the much maligned George III, so harassed by politics and politicians, as also by his too large family. He was a good, respectable man, anxious to do his duty. Richard saw that, with his largely German background, he wished to reward merit, when English aristocrats regarded themselves as qualified for any job they fancied. ('No damned merit about it,' said Lord Melbourne of the Order of the Garter.) I noticed that, when George III pushed in John Moore as Archbishop of Canterbury, a good man, but a grazier's son.

Nobody notices what a patron of the arts the King was, of painters and painting and science, with his personal interest in astronomy and encouragement of Herschel, greatest of astronomers at the time. The King himself was the leading book collector (except for Richard Heber), his library forming the nucleus of the British Museum. He loved music, carrying on the family devotion to Handel. All this interests me more than the ins-and-outs of politics, though Pares's last book, *George III and the Politicians*, was devoted to them. He saw that to a lot of them it was a game, and some of them played it 'for fun'. Richard thought that one reason for the extraordinary quarrelsomeness of eighteenth century politicians was that they enjoyed too rich a diet, ate too much meat and drank too much port. George III lived on a simple low diet, was abstemious and lived long. The great Lord Chatham would not take the King's advice on this. His fool of a doctor prescribed pounds and pounds of roast beef and gallons of port, while the great man grew madder and madder.

Pares understood the mysterious, misunderstood personality of the younger Pitt as no one has done. A clue was that he turned after his mother's family, the Grenvilles. We mostly think of him as a statue in the Abbey; few penetrate – or were allowed to penetrate – beneath the surface. Everybody spoke of the charm of Charles James Fox. But, if ever Pitt could take time off from the pressure of affairs for a weekend in the country, a chosen few saw that the younger man had quite as much charm, was irresistible even to opponents. We know only the public man, leader of his country, and indeed of Europe for much of twenty years of crises and wars let loose by the French Revolution and Napoleon. Pitt was a man of peace. When he died, utterly worn out at forty-six, his grand opponent, Fox, uttered a classic epitaph: 'It seemed as if there were something missing in the world.'

Pares was booked to write the Reign of George III in the new Oxford History of England. What a fine work he would have made of it! But he was now beyond it. For the last year or two of his life he was totally paralysed, all but his head – though what a brilliant piece that was! I used to feed him his lunch on Mondays and Thursdays; and on Thursdays push him round Oxford in his wheelchair. Summer afternoons we would sit out under the whitebeam, between the buttresses of the Codrington Library. There I read to him the eighteenth century chapters of my family history of the Churchills. He had not much to criticise, but what he had to fill in about the background was always enlightening.

Once we were almost stranded in the great garden of Trinity, a snowfield all round us. A most romantic scene, but we were alone and the wheels of his chair were blocked with snow, hard to start up again. It made me think of Richard's Russian background. As a child in Russia he had spoken Russian, though this had faded.

Pares's *George III and the Politicians* contained his Ford Lectures. Oddly enough, he thought that to give them was 'the highest honour which an English historian can receive'. (Many second-rate lectures have been given under that heading.)

Richard was carried up all those steps in his wheelchair by some tough young men. The Examination Schools had been a

146

hospital during the wars – and yet nobody had thought of installing a lift in the vast 'Anglo-Jackson' building. These were Richard's last public appearances as a lecturer, and fine performances they were. At the end of the first McFarlane had to go up to Richard and correct a minimal slip – so like him.

These lectures exhibit all Richard's characteristics of mind: brilliant, amusing, full of common sense, no illusions about anything, least of all politics and politicians. By now he had taken their score in Whitehall. The tone is singularly *désabusé*, as befits the eighteenth century, and yet not cynical at bottom. 'It would be wrong to infer that [their] politics was an utterly sordid affair. That it was not, even for the careerists. They wished, as very few of us do not, to leave the world a richer place than they had entered it.' This seems to me positively idealistic.

He concluded that the professionals, as against the amateurs, were 'all men of business, fascinated by the details of policy and administration – trade, revenue, and the reform of administrative machinery'. I think that that spoke for him too. 'It is a pity that historians should so seldom have recognised the fact that men were in politics not only for party and for profit, but most of all for the due exercise of the talents God gave them, and for fun.'

The book as such is thick with the hair-splitting differences as to constitutional rights and conventions between Crown and Parliament, the subtle shifts in balance of power, the self-justifications of everybody. I prefer to dispense with all that mumbo-jumbo beloved of the academic mind. As Pares himself says, 'The differences were personal, but the constitutional history of this country is made up of personal differences. The decline of personal monarchy was, in part, a personal decline.'

Very well then – enough.

There is always a certain development going on, with changing circumstances, and this is largely inevitable – in the longer run, if not in the shorter. Pares himself concludes, 'The conditions of political life were changing, and the power of the Crown was not what it had been.'

It is enough then to say that George III stood for the past, what the rights of the Crown were, while Charles James Fox stood for the future, what these would become under erosion. We might say the same in regard to Charles I's conflict with his Parliament: he stood for the past, the rights of the Crown as he had inherited them, Parliament for the future, evolutionary development.

That is enough to my mind.

Sir Bernard Pares was widely known as our chief expert on Russian affairs. He was so much in love with Russia that he was always wanting to be there, and he neglected the family. They were unhappy. At one time husband and wife would communicate with each other only through the intermediary of their eldest boy. Richard thought, from his boyhood, that adult humans were fools. As a boy he used to be sent down to 10 Downing Street to play in the garden with the Prime Minister's youngest, 'Puffin' Asquith.

Richard wrote of the younger Pitt that 'a boy shut up for hours with a daemonic father like the Earl of Chatham could only hope to defend himself if he could parry thought by thought with the speed of lightning.' I saw something of this when Sir Bernard stayed at All Souls, and how much he encouraged, and enjoyed, Richard's quickness of mind. (I envied him having such a father.)

At Harrow Bernard Pares had had for room-mate Stanley Baldwin, but could recall nothing distinctive about him. This was the leading politician in the decadence of Britain – to which he so largely contributed – between the two wars.

The elder Pares had not begun as an historian. He was a professor of Russian language and literature. As such he made a virtuoso translation of Krylov's *Fables*, reproducing the Russian metrics and rhyme scheme. He also wrote a journalistic account of his many Days in Russia. It was only as an old man that he wrote his best books. *The Fall of the Russian Monarchy* is remarkable for he knew many of the leading characters, the Tsar Nicholas II and his wife, an Anglophile couple, the Empress a fatal liability, comparable to Marie Antoinette. Pares spent the three years of war, 1914 to 1917, in Russia and witnessed the February Revolution. He knew Kerensky and many of the Liberals, was a friend of their leader, Milyukov.

We were so beglamoured by Lenin and the Bolshevik Revolution that we discounted Bernard Pares's views. His best book was his big History of Russia. When I reread it recently I was abashed to find how right he had been about Communism, long before the rest of us, much more foresighted, and how remarkable his belief that things would come round again and Russia right herself. He saw that Lenin's Revolution distorted the proper, popular course of Russian history. Today we can see, though belatedly, how much happier for Russia if it had never happened.

Richard, with his almost inhumanly exacting standards, was forced to admit that his father had been a good historian after all.

CHAPTER 21

Samuel Eliot Morison

Morison was the greatest of American historians. Of my two friends I used to think happily of them dividing the honours equally, Trevelyan at the head of the profession in Britain, Morison in the United States. They had many characteristics in common: rock-like endurance, intellectual integrity, candour and clarity, downrightness. They made no compromises, and they had no scepticism; both were dedicated literary artists.

I have come to realise that Morison had the wider range and longer pull. Not only the tract of American history to compare with Trevelyan's on Britain, a more elongated record, but Morison's many books on maritime history – fifteen volumes on the US Navy in the Second World War! Then he made a contribution to intellectual history, with four volumes on Harvard and the Intellectual Life of Colonial New England. There were also biographies and charming booklets of autobiography. Morison had a longer active life, and the achievement was prodigious.

He too was born in the purple, a comparable strain of intellectual aristocracy – Eliots, Otises, Roots, Nortons – but the high-and-dry New England strain was fertilised by an Irish streak from Baltimore, a warmer, more sensitive clime. Hence his greater breadth and freedom of expression; an unquestioned stylist, with a good grounding in the classics and English literature, he could write colloquially, and I love his exceptional, often nautical, vocabulary. He was a lifelong sailing man.

As a young man Morison came over from Harvard to be our first Professor of American History at Oxford and tell us what was what. There he spent three of the happiest years of his life, and Christ Church became his second home. Though an undergraduate there at the time, I was not made aware of him. The dons were not favourable to American history, and they thought Sam brash.

He was quite right to be challenging. Wasn't it far more important to learn about American history than about the seals and signets of the Middle Ages, to which I was directed by my tutor, E.F. Jacob? (*Savoir tout, ce n'est pas Tout pardonner.*)

Reading Sam's Inaugural Address now, after seventy years, I find that it can hardly be bettered as a statement of the case for his subject. He was downright, and he was right. Not a bit of anti-English feeling, for all the sore issues between the two countries which history raised – and he was a patriot. Not a trace of inferiority complex – indeed it might well be said that he exhibited a superiority complex. In that like the English themselves.

I find his statement a model of open-mindedness and justice of mind, that rarest of qualities. We can now see that the American Revolution, the breach between the mother country and the colonies, was one of the tragedies of history. The tragedy was that America's achievement of nationhood – inevitable as it was – should have come about through war, exacerbated by a second war, 1812–14. It left a legacy of distrust and anti-British feeling, of which the embers have not been wholly extinguished today. Americans have never forgotten that the White House was burned, and that crack British regiments, under the command of a stupid Pakenham, were mown down, to give Andrew Jackson a victory at New Orleans.

It is true that no power in the eighteenth century would have let go of their colonies, and everybody thought that the loss of Britain's would be her end as a power. Nevertheless, the best political brains in Britain – the Pitts and Foxes, Burke, Shelburne – were all pro-American. It was the blinkered mentality of back-benchers that kept the struggle going – like that which backed Chamberlain through the years of Appeasement (he was anti-American too, on top of everything else). Why couldn't the followers of Chatham and Rockingham, who were right about America, have joined together before it was too late? – Because of party politics and personalities.

I used to raise a laugh from American audiences by teasing them that it was all very well for them to complain of the insolence of the aristocrats – but they were three thousand miles away: we had them to put up with on the doorstep. It was understandable that they should find the rabble-rousers of Boston, such types as Sam Adams, too provoking – and Massachusetts was always ungovernable.

Morison wrote that 'the English Colonies of North America were founded in great part as a protest against the England of the Stuarts. The Puritans emigrated largely to save certain English ideals and ways of living that they deemed most precious and which they could no longer realise in England.' In fact, they went over there to get their own way – naturally enough; when they got there they showed themselves no more tolerant than Archbishop Laud, in truth a good deal less.

It was natural that Morison, with his background, should idealise the New England Puritans – and there were fine men among them, Governor Bradford of the Pilgrim Fathers, who write a good history of the Plymouth Colony; the first John Winthrop, Governor of the Bay Colony, i.e. Massachusetts. Morison found these people even lovable. I could not. He inscribed the book he gave me, *By Land and Sea*, 'Still hoping to educate him about the Puritans.' It amused me that he should line up with Trevelyan about them.

I was already sufficiently educated about the Puritans. How could one like a society that had no drama, no theatre or opera; no cathedrals, no sculpture or stained glass; no music to speak of, except their old Puritan hymns; for literature, endless theological nonsense and sermons? As a schoolboy, I had always loved Nathaniel Hawthorne – I don't think that the author of *The Scarlet Letter* liked the Puritans, any more than Walter Scott liked the Covenanters.

Fairness compels me to admit that Puritanism was a prime element in the backbone of the nation. Can one perhaps have too much backbone? I recall an old ramrod of a New England dowager fixing me with, 'I don't want to hate anybody [she didn't try hard enough], but I must uphold *Virtue*' – clacking her dentures minatorily. I used to think of Sam as a piece of old Plymouth Rock – that head sculpted in granite; and recalled Chesterton's, 'We hear so much of the Pilgrim Fathers landing on Plymouth Rock – would that Plymouth Rock had landed on the Pilgrim Fathers!'

On a purely professional point, Morison's perspective was that of New England, in the making of the nation. But the colonisation of Virginia began a whole generation before the great emigration to Massachusetts in the 1630s. I gave the first Trevelyan Lectures at Cambridge on *The Elizabethans and America*, specifically to correct this perspective. I saw the southern colonisation as the extrapolation of the Elizabethan age, the culmination of the earlier efforts of Ralegh, Grenville, John White, and the propaganda of Hakluyt, rather than the exodus of the godly to their new Jerusalem, 'set, as it were, upon an hill, to lighten the earth'. Anyway, Richard Pares used to provide me with snippets from Increase Mather about the goings-on in the earthly paradise – the sexual irregularities and deviations, examples of rustic bestiality. The godly were a minority even in Massachusetts – still more so in reprobate old England.

Neither Trevelyan nor Morison could make me love the Puritans.

A product of Morison's time at Christ Church was his *Oxford History of the United States*, the first of his histories of his people. I cannot sufficiently praise his grasp of the vast, sprawling, *lateral* subject. It is the fairness of mind, breadth of sympathies, generosity – the best American characteristics – that stand out all through his work. He had a phrase that goes to the root of the matter: 'History is to the community what memory is to the individual.' Where would humans be without memory? The subject needs no further defence. But the *appeal* is that 'the story of mankind, with all his nobility and baseness, wisdom and folly, is the most interesting and fascinating of stories'. Here was a romantic strain, as with Trevelyan, and both could communicate it, for both were literary artists, without however being aesthetes.

'In a sense, all American history is the story of westward expansion.' Here was the clue – F.J. Turner's 'Frontier Thesis', of which we used to hear far too much – without subjecting everything to its strait-jacket. (Turner could write about nothing else.) Since this westward advance was the most characteristic movement of the nineteenth century, I think he found it the most significant in the story. It is certainly the most romantic – and the most tragic, with the terrible epic of the Civil War, or the War between the States, as unreconstructed Southerners will have it to be.

For all its heroism and touching characters, on both sides, it was a thousand pities that ever it was fought. Again, it was a profound mistake on the part of the South to challenge the North with three times its resources, population, naval ascendancy, etc. Again, if the South had not fought so heroically, the conflict would not have lasted so long, or done so much irretrievable harm. People do not reflect what a loss it made to the United States as a whole that the contribution of the South was withdrawn, mutely missing for half a century. Not until Woodrow Wilson was there a Southern President again.

Once more, my ambivalent sympathies would have been with the neutrals, such as the Cornish Senator Foote, of Alabama, who, defeated, withdrew from the conflict – as Hobbes did before the English Civil War. Indeed, I have gone so far as to wonder, if Abraham Lincoln had not been elected, there might have been no war. The South took his election as a declaration of war. With a compromise candidate could a compromise have been patched up, and gone on and on ... until, by the end of the century, slavery would surely have worn itself out?

Such sceptical thoughts would never recommend themselves to Trevelyan any more than to Morison. Both men were straight and simple, more in line with normal mankind. Morison treats the war as the brave conflict it was, more devastating in its casualties than any other in the century – thus all the more regrettable to my unheroic mind.

Lincoln was of course his hero, 'almost broken by the burden of a war that he loathed to the depth of his soul, yet never losing his humanity and his humility, buoyed up by Christian faith and a sense of humour: the supreme product of democracy.' In fact, Lincoln was not a Christian believer – Morison was; Lincoln seems to have been an undogmatic Rationalist. Humility? – if that is a virtue. Lincoln was extremely ambitious, anxious for the Presidency, and knew his own value.

So great an historic figure does not need any defence in conventional terms. I once teased an unreconstructed Southern young lady in Richmond, the capital of the Confederacy, by recommending him as of Southern descent. 'Then wasn't he the least bit of a traitor?' said she. There was the old Southern spirit. My oldest American friend, another Southerner, on our Sunday walks away from the Huntington Library, would refight the Civil War. The South would win; since we were liberal-minded, slavery would be abolished – except that we would enslave Harriet Beecher Stowe.

Before Oxford Morison had already written the *Life and Letters of Harrison Gray Otis*, a work of family piety. The great name in the family was James Otis, a leader of Opposition in Massachusetts. Loyalists imputed this to his father's having been beaten for the Chief Judgeship by Thomas Hutchinson, who as Governor advised the British government badly as to the state of opinion in the province. An able lawyer, Otis made a fortune out of land speculation after the Revolution. The Otis House was just down the street from Sam's family home in Boston, 44 Brimmer Street. America's population is volatile, apt to be rootless. 'A house that has sheltered the same family for a century is a curiosity.'

He had also written the *Maritime History of Massachusetts*, in which he was no less at home. From his boyhood – and there always remained something boyish and naif about him – he had been mad about boats and sailing; in time he was to become a very expert seaman. 'In the Boston shipyards was perfected the noblest and swiftest sailing-vessel of all time, the Yankee clipper ship, stately as a cathedral, beautiful as a terraced cloud, the wonder and the joy of man as she swept around the Horn to 'Frisco, around the Cape to Melbourne, smashing every record for every trade route.'

Here was Sam's aesthetic, here and in the beauty of women, for whom he expressed an old-fashioned gallantry. (Nothing of that in Trevelyan). One might say that he was a very manly man, bent on challenging his seamen at their own game and skills.

He was also an intellectual – that was what was odd. There followed at least four books on the founding and record of Harvard. There had been some thirty-five Emmanuel men from Cambridge, eleven of them Fellows. Morison was not restricted to those original sympathies, and even Harvard was theologically broad enough to send a too strict contingent down the coast to found Yale. Thank goodness, Harvard was not all theology, it developed a fine classical tradition as well.

Morison himself was well educated in the classics, he had that advantage over us – there was his father's fine library at 44 Brimmer Street to back him. To this he added his own equipment, Spanish and Portuguese, for his *Portuguese Voyages* into the North Atlantic, and for his books on Christopher Columbus. As a sailing man, he organised and led an expedition to follow, as far as possible, Columbus' track in similar conditions, a specially designed sailing vessel that was a replica of Columbus' ship, and of course Sam kept the log-book and published it. I am not competent to appreciate all this, but I read the splendid biography of Columbus that eventuated from it all.

On the intellectual front he was well aware that his American colleagues didn't write as well as himself. 'In the period between the two World Wars, I became exercised over the bad English used by students of history, especially graduate students, and over the dull pedantic manner in which many historical monographs were presented. There has been a sort of chain reaction of dullness. Professors who have risen to positions of eminence by writing dull, solid, valuable monographs that nobody reads outside the profession, teach graduate students to write dull, solid, valuable [?] monographs like theirs.' This was the road to academic security.

Morison knew well that this came partly through the German

cult of the Ph.D. which prevailed in American universities in the later nineteenth century. Why? – when they had a far better tradition of their own, with gifted historians like Parkman and Prescott, or Washington Irving, to go no further back to the beginning with Governor Bradford or Berkeley. One may say that the situation has worsened with the prevalence of Political Correctness, except for a few notable exceptions like Alan Brinkley of (again) Harvard.

Morison himself set the best example. Why didn't they follow it? The simple answer is that they couldn't see it. I remember being enraged by a third-rate instructor in a college in the Middle West, who would *not* accept that Morison was an historian of the first rank. At length the numbskull had a burst of enlightenment: 'You only mean that he is a first-class *writer*.' At that I blew up: 'If you weren't so third-rate you'd be able to see that he is a first-rate historian.' It is a duty to confront such people with the truth.

At length, after over half a century of study, teaching and writing, Morison produced a really great book, of over a thousand pages, the *Oxford History of the American People*. 'Politics are not lacking; but my main ambition is to re-create American ways of living in bygone eras. Social and economic developments, horses [he was a rider from boyhood], popular sports and pastimes; eating, drinking, and smoking habits. Pugilists will be found cheek-by-jowl with Presidents, rough-necks with reformers, artists with ambassadors. More, proportionally, than in other histories, will be found on sea power, on the colonial period in which basic American principles were established, on the Indians and the Caribbean.' He even annexed in parallel, if briefly, the history of Canada, 'so near and dear to us, yet so unknown in her historical development to most citizens of the United States'.

'Having lived through several critical eras, dwelt or sojourned in every section of our country, taken part in both world wars, met and talked with almost every President of the United States in the 20th century, as well as with thousands of men and women active in various pursuits, I have reached some fairly definite opinions about our history.'

He had indeed, and Sam was not one for hiding their light under a bushel. This frank expression of personality, which made his books live, did not endear him within the profession. Though he had a vast public outside, he was not popular inside.

I was present at a tell-tale scene in that famous library at 44 Brimmer Street. Sam had just come back from a consultation with President Truman in Washington, and of course he had to tell his colleagues that he had been down to see the 'Great White Chief'. They affected not to know whom he meant, and looked to me to enjoy his embarrassment. My sympathies were entirely with him – I knew their sort only too well.

Since this great work was not a textbook but intended for the general reader Morison took some risks – the old seaman was never afraid of taking a risk. He omitted footnotes and any *apparatus criticus*. More oddly, at the end of many chapters appeared a couple of bars of music. No serious history had sported that kind of thing before. For years Sam had been collecting the songs of the people – he had quite a folksy line, not only in that. He was very sentimental about his second wife, Priscilla, a cousin from Baltimore, a singer, and she helped him with the chanties.

Sam thought that often one of the people's songs summed up a period or gave it its theme. No doubt. In music one can breathe the air of a vanished age, hear its heartbeat as its denizens did. As with 'Greensleaves' one can *hear* the pulse of the Elizabethan age, so with 'Shenandoah', one of the most haunting tunes ever invented. Or, as one is gathered round the piano in a Virginian homestead, to hear the old songs of Dixie, one enters into the spirit of the Confederacy, better than the flags on all the Capitols of the Old South.

In England this marvellous book was attacked by a young Cambridge academic, who had not written anything himself, nor was to. Indignant at this, I sent him a rocket. It did no good: I don't think he could even *see* the grandeur of conception and execution. Sam wrote to me that he didn't mind. What he minded was his colleagues over there forever picking on 'picayune' errors. Evidently he *was* sensitive to criticism, as Trevelyan – who took no notice, and never entered into controversy – was not.

*

With America's entry into the Second World War, after Pearl
Harbor, the elderly professor got his chance of service at sea. I
knew little of that, except that we had a common friend in
Admiral Nimitz, who took over the command at Pearl Harbor
after the disaster: a noble fellow, third-generation German from
the Texan Panhandle. Sam was proud of being on board of a
warship under Japanese kamikaze bombing – and boasted of it.
(Why shouldn't he?)

After the war he was allotted the task of writing the History of
US Naval Operations in both the Atlantic and the Pacific. An
individualist, perhaps something of a monopolist, he accomplished this with the minimum of help. I have been in the little
carel in the Houghton Library at Harvard, where he wrote most
of it, with room for only one assistant.

Of all fifteen volumes I have read in only one or two, notably
that on the battle of Midway Island, when the whole balance of
sea-power in the Pacific was turned, in twenty minutes, with the
sinking of four Japanese aircraft-carriers. I have met the victor,
Admiral Spruance, a grizzled, pepper-and-salt colour Scotch
type – a silent man, 'terrifically aggressive', according to Nimitz.

Nimitz, who was a humane, civilised man, told me sadly that
the victory had been at the expense of all his fighter pilots, save
one. This fellow got into his rubber dinghy, and the battle of
Midway Island was fought all round him. He survived, and
corresponded regularly with the Admiral from his home in the
East. Nimitz carried a tremendous burden of correspondence
from all over the States, replying by hand – so that he could
never write up his own Memoirs. Sam kept in touch with him
regularly, as I did, more conveniently from the Huntington
Library, since the Admiral lived practically on the campus at
Berkeley.

For his outsize work for the US Navy Morison was made a
Rear-Admiral. Henceforth no more Professor, always Rear-
Admiral S.E. Morison. Nor did this render him more endearing
to academic colleagues. For all his democratic convictions, and
they were genuine, the old piece of Plymouth Rock did not suffer

fools gladly. This was not popular. (Why should one?) On a later visit to Oxford, some women pressed forward in the line to say, 'I am such an admirer of your books!' Sam said loudly, 'Which one?' Of course she couldn't remember a single one. At meetings of the American Historical Association, Sam was reported as saying, 'I extended the glad hand.' He was no more given to humbug than Trevelyan was.

Like him, Morison was a generous man. He paid tribute to Charles Beard's *Rise of American Civilisation* for more than it was worth: Beard was the Prophet of the Politically Correct in his day, and this book was their gospel (it was recommended to me by Harold Laski). When one came to his later work, on President Roosevelt's Foreign Policy, one saw the crapulousness of his judgement, with its regular technique of innuendo.

'Beard could see no menace to the United States if Hitler conquered all Europe, and Japan took the other half of the world, suppressing liberty as they proceeded.' Beard gave a lead to Left Isolationists by suggesting that Roosevelt knew of the impending attack on Pearl Harbor. Beard had another pro-German professor-follower, who did not hesitate to go further, and virtually suggested that at Pearl Harbor it was the Americans who attacked the Japanese! One really *sickens* at such people. Sam did not: he took it all with good humour in a piece 'History through a Beard'. Perhaps that annoyed them all the more.

The Rear-Admiral continued on his independent way, impertur-bably, with his cruising at Mount Desert and off the coast of Maine, and with his writings about the sea. With his *John Paul Jones* he did a remarkable job. Hitherto, Paul Jones had been an American folk-hero about whom legends clustered and there was little certainty. Sam went into action, with his nose for research, and cleared up that doubtful career. The American privateer, who created alarm, if not despondency, around the coasts of Britain during the Revolutionary War, was really a Scot. He made history with his *Bonhomme Richard*, named for Benjamin Franklin's popular almanac, *Poor Richard*. Paul

Jones operated out of Brest, and his success against odds was phenomenal. New England privateers were quite the equals of their opposite numbers. Same stock.

Sam followed this with short autobiographical books which I find enchanting. *The Story of Mount Desert Island, Maine* combines history with seamanship, folklore, sea-lore – those reefs and rocks and dangerous channels. He had initiated Priscilla into those sea-ways as his mate on board. Her story appears in *Spring Tides*. *One Boy's Boston* has a nostalgic charm, recapturing that of a vanished society, more agreeably to my mind than Henry James's *The Bostonians*. Henry James was an outsider, from New York – as was Isabella Stewart Gardner, the most glittering figure in that world. I can only sigh with envy at how lucky Sam was to have grown up in that world, the security, the complacency of it, with its high standards of culture. Boston before the Flood! It offers a contrast to the depiction of it by Santayana, whose 'delicate nostrils' Sam politely deplored.

Santayana, a pure Spaniard, did not like that still Puritan ethos. Though he is a favourite with me, Sam's account, as an insider, is the more authentic. He was an Eliot. He told me that he had worked out his relationship to T.S. Eliot: they enjoyed the same relationship as President Franklin Roosevelt to President Teddy Roosevelt – they were seventh cousins.

In his eighties Morrison settled for yet one more great work, *The European Discovery of America*. This took two stout volumes, first, the Northern Voyages, second, the Southern Voyages. He was not content to review all the written evidence in all the languages, but to check them on the ground, from Greenland and Labrador around the Caribbean to Cape Horn. He was insatiable. He travelled by ship, by plane, helicopter, motor-boat, whatever was necessary to get to the exact spot. He was helped on his voyages of exploration, now a famous Rear-Admiral, by the navies of the USA and Great Britain, as well as of Brazil, Chile and others.

He wrote as uncompromisingly as ever. 'It has fallen to my lot, working on this subject, to have read some of the most tiresome historical literature in existence. Young men seeking academic promotion, old men seeking publicity, neither one nor the other knowing the subject in depth, write worthless articles. Some of these stem from mere personal conceit, others from racial emotion. Canada and the United States seem to be full of racial groups who seek to capture the "real" for their medieval compatriots.'

It is much like the crackpots writing about Shakespeare, Marlowe, Bacon, the erratic Earl of Oxford.

'My knowledge of seafaring, acquired over a period of seventy years, enables me to stretch back across the centuries and understand not only the triumphs of the navigators but their day-by-day problems.' Climate, weather, tides, reefs, maps. 'Dozens of islands, rocks and shoals that do not, and never did, exist are depicted on charts of the Atlantic, even down to the 19th century.'

With his second volume, on the Southern Voyages, 'now I return to Columbus, of whom I have been an almost lifelong student ... In the 1930s I followed Columbus across the Atlantic and around the West Indies in barquentine *Capitana* and ketch *Mary Otis* to write *Admiral of the Ocean Sea* and *Christopher Columbus, Mariner*.' He thought Columbus greatest of them all – Magellan, Drake, Gilbert, John Davis: he could have settled any time for a castle in Spain, or a pension from Court, but he always wanted to go one more. Just like Sam.

'T.S. Eliot's injunction in his *East Coker*, "Old men ought to be explorers", has appealed to me; and I would add, "Young historians too!" ' It was a good thing that this great man did not survive to read the reams of rubbish written *against* Columbus, by the third-rate Politically Correct at the recent Quincentenary. What is so tell-tale about them all is that they cannot bear what is first-rate, excellence in any form, greatness of any kind. To do them justice, they cannot understand it – out of their reach.

Sam Morison was a democrat, he was also an empire-builder: in his work he built a fabulous empire. In announcing his programme in beginning at Oxford he wrote, 'We who study American history shall be creating the future out of that past; not only for America, but for all peoples who aspire to a better life.' Today all peoples, for better or worse, aspire to Americanisation.

CHAPTER 22

Allan Nevins

Allan Nevins was the most widely known American historian of his time – more so than Sam Morison, and on a rather lower level. For, though Morison accomplished a mountain of work, Nevins produced, unbelievably, three or four times as much. Fifty full-length books, a dozen or so short ones, a hundred volumes which he edited, innumerable newspaper articles and reviews. Everybody regarded him as a prodigy. He was, rather, an automaton: he ran mechanically, like clockwork.

Quantity, Quantity – he had not the *quality* of Morison. I always assessed him as 6 + + + ... *ad infinitum*. He had not been born in the Bostonian purple, with the background of Harvard – he rather resented that. A farm-boy from Illinois, he had come up the hard way, and made it through journalism in New York. This training meant that he wrote not only more prolifically but better than American academics in general. Though pedestrian, he was at least readable: he knew how to write a book.

He was my oldest American friend. I first met him at Oxford between the wars. In the 1960s we were colleagues for several years as Senior Research Associates at the Huntington Library in California. I owed to him my introduction into the intimacy of American family life, where for long I felt an outsider. Englishmen think that they understand America without difficulty, because of the sameness of language. In fact America is very hard to understand; for ages it baffled me – it baffles Americans themselves. It took me years to get the hang of it. I have been in nearly every State in the Union – more than most Americans can say. I found Allan's talk, during lunch-time breaks at the Huntington – he had no other time to spare –

invaluable, especially when I came to write my book on *The Cornish in America*. Allan was a walking American encyclopedia.

The Americans were unaware of the Cornish folk in their midst. Allan made the point that, if only the Cornish had produced a Robert Burns, people would have been aware of them. But the Cornish were miners, not poets. Nor were they politicians, like the Irish, always on their hind legs making trouble. They were quiet folk, who melted happily into the background.

It is out of the question to cite Allan's vast *oeuvre*, let alone do justice to it – anyway I was unaware of most of it. I had found his *Brief History of the United States* useful, partly because it was short and published at Oxford. It served a similar purpose for students as my short *Spirit of English History*.

Allan was an old-fashioned American liberal, an Anglophile, who was religiously addicted to the former *Manchester Guardian*. He therefore imputed Europe's troubles to the Treaty of Versailles, and subscribed to ignorant Revisionism. Nicholas Roosevelt had lived in Central Europe as ambassador to Hungary and understood perfectly well that Germany's grievance was that she had lost the war. When Mr Roosevelt came to visit us, he and I understood the source of the trouble: we saw eye to eye, and no need to consider Allan's naif Revisionism. We both ignored it.

Allan swallowed whole the Robbins Report on British universities. The ablest woman at Oxford, Lucy Sutherland, Principal of Lady Margaret Hall, dismissed it shortly as 'nonsense'. A most distinguished of provincial university professors regards it as having done 'untold damage' to our universities. Robbins himself said to me, when we received honorary degrees together at Exeter, that he favoured the inflation of such institutions, 'provided we realise that they are second-rate'. Agreed – but did we need so many third-rate ones?

Allan not only fell for the Robbins Report but actually tried to *make* me subscribe to it. No one can force me to say what I do not believe, and an almighty row ensued over the Christmas lunch-table at the Coronado Hotel at Point Loma. He had no idea that the question of *Quality* in university education was crucial. He genuinely was unable to see the point: with him it was Quantity, Quantity all the way.

He received a rude awakening from the students themselves, with their sit-ins, the damage they did on so many campuses all over the United States – as also to a lesser extent in Britain, though bad enough at such places as Essex University. At Allan's own university, Columbia, they burned the fine Law Library. That taught him. There were too many university students already, and in the USA uneducated up to any university standard. *Their* problem was really with school education – it still is. (And here?)

Allan dreamed too the American dream. He thought that the United States had a God-given mission to bring enlightenment to the bad Old World. This was the kind of thing that enraged a really educated European like de Gaulle: he thought it callow, and insufferably patronising from an uneducated source. Meanwhile, Vietnam educated them as to the facts of human nature. Jefferson's illusions about democracy and men's rationalism simply did not apply. Before Allan retired from the Huntington I did a little in the way of re-educating him.

Once I was present when an emissary came from Berkeley, where the campus was in uproar and university work suspended. Allan asked what was it that the students wanted, what were their needs and interests? What were they discussing? The young lady thought for a moment, and then replied naively, 'They only discussed campus politics.' I laughed to myself, but left the report to do its work on Allan.

He was so Anglophile in his sympathies that once, when we were discussing the American Revolution, he surprised me by saying that it would have been better if the colonies had emerged with Dominion Status. But surely that could never have worked? The wide open spaces of America were far too large. Manifest Destiny called, the Revolution dispensed with the protection the British government desiderated for the Indians, and the Americans spilled relentlessly ever westward. No government in London could have held up their progress.

Once, when Harold Nicolson was lecturing in America, a lady

do-gooder kept chipping in with How about our treatment of the Indians? Until Harold said, 'Do you mean our treatment of our Indians, or *your* treatment of *your* Indians?' Best thing he ever said.

Allan received commissions to write the official biographies of several of the great tycoons of industry, J.D. Rockefeller, Ford, etc. This was an awkward assignment for an American Liberal. He said to me, defensively, that if it had not been for their fortunes, many of the beneficent foundations that are a great ornament of American society would not have come into being – Rockefeller, Guggenheim, Lehmann, Wrightson, Ford, etc.

I read the first volume of his *Rockefeller*, who needed no defence for me. It was obviously right to force the amalgamation of hundreds of individual gushers pouring out oil and wasting it in streams. Ford, who thought 'History is all Bunk', had no appeal for me. When the man came to Oxford he had no interest in the historic scene, but couldn't wait to see Morris's motor-works at Cowley. I expect he would approve the former notice at the railway station: 'Oxford – the place where Morris cars are made.' By this time History has declared Ford, with his Nazi sympathies, to be Bunk.

Allan was not invited to write the rather complicated story of Henry E. Huntington. Not all the researchers who enjoyed his benefaction at his library were grateful, though I was mindful of it every day in the beautiful place he created. Grace Hubble, widow of the eminent astonomer, friend of Aldous Huxley, had a special permit to walk in the gardens after they were closed. Glimpsing the family at dinner – candlelight, Louis XVI furniture, French tapestries, footmen – 'I felt like throwing a rock through the window,' said she. So much for the taste of the liberal intelligentsia.

Allan had had a hand in helping forward President Kennedy's *Profiles in Courage*. The day he was assassinated Allan had the typescript of a further Kennedy book in his office. We were all appalled by the news coming over – I remember the scene on the terrace well, and how we all trooped off at noon to service in All

Saints church. Allan said to me, 'I shall never take the same interest in politics again.' There was the reaction of the typical American liberal. And then, 'The instinct of democracy is to *lop the tallest.*'

They had lopped Lincoln. Allan was forever writing about him and the Civil War: *The Ordeal of the Union*, two volumes, *The Emergence of Lincoln*, two volumes, *The War for the Union*, four volumes, *The Statesmanship of the Civil War*, and more besides. He had none of the statesmanlike grasp of Morison, seeing both sides of the great divide. Allan was a simple, unreconstructed Northerner. To him the great soldier of the South, Churchill's hero, Robert E. Lee, was just 'a traitor to the United States'.

The cult of Lincoln, going on and on forever about him, was rather a bore. On one of the days sacred to his memory we used to go into Los Angeles for a celebratory lunch and sing his praises once again. I had nothing to contribute, until I realised that none of them knew what the name 'Lincoln' meant. Lin-dum-colonia: the settlement at the fort above the pool, which exactly describes the situation of the ancient city on its hill, one Roman gateway still *in situ*.

We were accompanied on these sanctified pilgrimages into down-town Los Angeles by another colleague, Ray Billington. In a way a disciple of Nevins, he was also an independent power in his own right, the leader in the school of Mid-West history. He wrote a big standard work, *Westward Expansion*, completely reliable scholarship, hugely informative, to me a specimen of lateral history: history in width rather than depth, following the nature of the subject.

Ray, like all the rest, adhered to the pattern set by American democracy. Nobody must appear different from anybody else, any ego must be suppressed, we must all be the same, think the same way. It was a middle-class culture, dreadfully boring, in a way stifling. This was the culture from which Henry James, Edith Wharton, Eliot, Santayana and the Americans whom I admired had fled to Europe.

The home-keeping variety were easy to tease, though I

minded my p's and q's, for I was bent on learning America – my American education – Henry James in reverse. Ray, whom his Irish wife thought 'a sheep in wolf's clothing', was strong against 'loners' (I was one) – one was supposed to muck in with the rest, be like the rest of them. What an idea! So one day I said to Ray, 'Wasn't Abraham Lincoln a loner?' That caught him on the hop. 'Oh, that was different,' he said lamely.

Allan's ideas were all of a similar conventionality. He could not accept Walt Whitman's homosexuality – against all the evidence. He would repeat the old cliché, Whitman 'was of the earth, earthy'. The imperceptiveness of ordinary heteros passes belief. Of course he would never have understood the subtlety of the relationship between the handsome Hawthorne and Herman Melville, the author of *Billy Budd*. He wasn't musical, so he was spared from knowing what was what about Aaron Copland and Leonard Bernstein; or the noble army of lesbian ladies, Willa Cather, Amy Lowell, Gertrude Stein. And what *was* what about Emily Dickinson?

Allan understood only what was straight and simple before his eyes. No wonder there is no Irony in American literature – an aristocratic trait. Nor that de Gaulle and the French resented being patronised by such a culture. Allan was anti-French, in spite of Lafayette and all that. Nor did he like Henry Adams, who spoke for me among American writers – at any rate, the author of *The Education of Henry Adams*, most unpredictable of all American books, not the anti-English author of the Presidencies of Madison and Monroe, with its hereditary New England bias.

However, Nevins was a good and generous friend of Britain, a lifelong friend, not only in her adversity. He made a cult of things Scottish – nothing was ever mentioned of the Jewish side coming from his mother. In his last years he became a Unitarian. One sees the offsetting advantage of that, along with the deliberate emphasis on the Scottish side, plaid ties, Aberdeen terriers, etc. But he was a generous friend to the Hebrew university in Israel, presenting them with books – as again at Oxford: he handed over all his books as Harmsworth Professor to Queen's College, which had made him a Fellow.

From Allan I picked up blameless bits of political folklore, part of my American education. Abraham Lincoln was surprised to learn that an English gentleman did not shine his own shoes. 'Who does them then?' the President asked. Senator Charles Sumner was not popular. A fellow Senator said that he would not be attending his funeral, but he approved of it. President Teddy Roosevelt had an irrepressible daughter Alice, 'Princess Alice'. 'I can govern the United States, *or* I can govern Alice. But I can't do both.' As an old lady, Alice Roosevelt Longworth said that she 'preferred a polygamist who monogs to a monogamist who polygs.' As for the wry and dry President Coolidge, he must have been 'weaned on a pickle'. A lady dining at the White House admired the splendid Sèvres on the table. 'Yes,' said the President, 'when we came in here, there was so much crockery we didn't need to bring in any of our own.'

For all his endless kindness and hospitality (he became a rich man from all those books, loaded with medals and prizes and honours), I was able to make him only a small return. I dedicated poems and a book to him, and I proposed him for an honorary degree at Oxford, the only time I had any success in that line. I failed when I proposed J.B. Priestley, and that exquisite writer Jules Supervielle – *they* had never heard of him. I only wish now that I had tried Montherlant on them. How Allan would have been shocked if he had known all that was to be known about Montherlant!

CHAPTER 23

Sir Reginald Coupland

Coupland was, along with Hancock, the most distinguished historian among the Empire and Commonwealth group at Oxford. A tutor in ancient history at Trinity, he had been recruited into this new field by that remarkable man, Lionel Curtis. More than a recruitment, it was a conversion by 'the Prophet'; henceforth Coupland dedicated his life and work to the Empire. As the Australian Oxonian, K.C. Wheare says, he was 'an old-fashioned liberal imperialist' with a strong strain of idealism. He succeeded Curtis as Beit Lecturer in Colonial History, and then H.E. Egerton as Professor. With Egerton and Sir Francis Doyle, All Souls had an early stake in Colonial and American history.

Coupland was a prolific and excellent writer. He began with a good biography of Wilberforce, emancipator of slaves. The book had been published by the University Press, and then left to wither, like Rousseau's putative children on the steps of the Foundling Hospital. I got Odham's to republish it, when it achieved a good circulation and made the Professor several hundred pounds.

He built himself a rather grand house on the slopes of Boar's Hill, which we used to call 'the palazzo', since it was large enough to entertain the colonial governors whose society Coupland much affected. He took a practical hand in their work. This was not much liked by those academics *pur sang*, E.L. Woodward and Richard Pares, who wanted to turn All Souls into an ordinary academic institution of the usual kind.

Pares should have known better. No love was lost between Woodward and Coupland, who had overheard the 'Abbé'

170

Woodward telling me a *risqué* story at dinner in Hall one Sunday night. I was not shocked, but Coupland was, a prim Wykehamist ('Manners maketh man'). This put the Abbé rather at a disadvantage, and gave Coupland the edge in their feuding. Both were a bit pompous in their respective arks, and I was much amused. My sympathies were wholly with Coupland. Colonial governors and visitors from overseas were much more interesting than dons who were all too familiar. Actually, Coupland wrote better than the pure spirits, Woodward and Pares. And Coupland followed up swiftly, book after book, while they were much slower off the mark.

A book on *The American Revolution and the British Empire*, and another on *The Quebec Act* of 1774, gave rise to some criticism across the Atlantic. I don't know what they objected to, but both Americans and Canadians were tetchy. The Quebec Act had properly given the Catholic Church in Quebec toleration for is denizens, the great majority, and some privileges. The Puritans of New England had long feared the 'infectious hand of a bishop' – the Act was made a grievance, part of the propaganda of the intolerant New Englanders leading to the American Revolution. After it, the Canadian grievance was that Britain had conceded too much of Canadian territory to the Americans; while the American grievance was that they wanted more. In politics it is impossible to satisfy everybody.

Coupland next wrote a short biography of Stamford Raffles. Raffles was a wonderful young civil servant in India – impossible to do him justice here. In the course of the war against Napoleon, who had taken over Holland, Britain took over the Dutch possession of Java. Young Raffles ruled it to its great benefit, ending forced labour, etc., but was frustrated at the peace by Britain handing back Java to the Dutch. (Who else would have done it?)

Raffles went on to select the site of what became Singapore, then a hardly inhabited island, to control the sea-routes eastward and become the greatest emporium in the area. Returning home ill, Raffles founded the Zoo, before dying at the age of forty-five. A creative and constructive empire-builder, he was very much my man. Studying him gave Coupland his first insight into India and the East, which he followed up to good effect. He paid a first visit to India on a Royal Commission on the Superior Civil Services, and largely wrote its Report (1923).

Next Coupland invaded East Africa with really original research. He had come upon a cache of documents which provided the foundation for three notable volumes: *Kirk on the Zambesi, East Africa and the Invaders, The Exploitation of East Africa*. African history has no allure for me – except for South Africa, with Bishop Colenso of Natal, and the Cornish miners on the Rand (two of my uncles are buried there). I do not go so far as Trevor-Roper, who as Regius Professor proclaimed, 'Blacks have no history' – a typical *ipse dixit*. We may say that with these books Coupland laid the foundations of East African history.

In an admirable account of Coupland's work* Professor Jack Simmons tells us that Sir John Kirk was British Consul at Zanzibar from 1873 to 1886, 'the chief agent in the establishment of British power in East Africa ... The history of East Africa itself was unwritten, and especially the curious history of the Zanzibar Sultanate.' Professor Simmons, the best judge, since he had worked with Coupland on these subjects, regards the second volume, *East Africa and its Invaders*, as his 'best single contribution to learning: a book of 550 pages, based almost entirely on original resources – in the Public Record Office and the India Office, at Zanzibar and Mauritius. It shows all Coupland's merits at their best: lucidity, vigour, earnestness, and a strong architectural sense that shaped the book well. There is a good narrative too ... the second half dominated by a great Arab, Seyyid Said.'

Some years later he topped up these works with a moving account of *Livingston's Last Journey*. 'His study of East African history had shown him how great a part Livingstone had played in the destruction of the slave trade there.'

In 1936–37 Coupland served on the Royal Commission on the ever-lively question of Palestine. Its Report, which again he

* In *Proceedings of the British Academy*, XLV.

largely wrote, recommended Partition between incoming Jews and Palestinian Arabs. The Report was not acted upon, but it seems that he was more far-seeing. People with different noses cannot get on with each other, it appears, even if there is no decipherable difference of colour.

During the Second War Coupland was much involved with Indian affairs. He went on two official visits, the second being that of the Cripps Mission. Cripps was empowered to offer the Indians virtually all they wanted, the reality of independence. This should have succeeded but for Gandhi, who first accepted, and then withdrew, aborting the Mission and all its well-intentioned work. Saints are nuisances.

Coupland wrote the account of it in *The Cripps Mission*, and followed it with two historical surveys: *The Indian Problem, 1833–1935* and *Indian Politics, 1936–1942*. I have no time for these distractions. Evidently Coupland was brought up again, as in Palestine, with the inability of peoples, adhering to different forms of belief, however irrational, to get on with each other: the fundamental rift between Hindu and Muslim, for which Britain was in no way responsible.

This attracted Coupland's attention, for a last phase, into the problems of Nationalism within the Commonwealth. He intended a complete Survey in several volumes. He was by now a tired man, exhausted by so much work. He managed to complete the first volume, on Welsh and Scottish Nationalism, just before his death.

He certainly had found a vocation in the tenure of the Beit Chair (a South African foundation) in all those years, 1920–1948. Oddly enough, Warden Pember, who was a Little Englander, tried to get rid of it. He felt himself somewhat overwhelmed by Milner's *Kindergarten*, and the Empire-Commonwealth group. So he took the opportunity of being a member of the University Statutory Commission to unload the chair on to Balliol. I was too junior at the time, but I did not agree. The Beit Chair was cognate with our other History foundations. The chair of French literature, foisted upon us instead, was not: that should have gone to Queen's, with its line in Modern Languages. However, Coupland made a lachrymose appeal in College Meeting, which was effective, and we kept him for life.

Professor Simmons sums up his work as historian: 'He opened up a whole new field of historical study in East Africa; he applied a trained historian's mind fruitfully to current political problems in Palestine and India; he displayed to Englishmen of his day the greatness of Wilberforce and Livingstone.' He was not only a good imperialist, but a lifelong liberal. Though prim and proper, he was rather proud of having behaved badly, as an undergraduate, at a meeting of Joe Chamberlain, who had wrecked the Liberal Party for a couple of decades by his defection over Home Rule. In a pause of the great man's speech in the Town Hall Coupland had shouted, 'Judas!'

As Professor he fostered and ran the Ralegh Club. As K.C. Wheare writes, its members were undergraduates chosen from Britain and other Commonwealth countries, who 'met on Sunday evenings in Rhodes House to hear and to discuss talks on imperial problems by visiting speakers. That the Ralegh Club could command such a galaxy of distinguished speakers from all over the world and that it could attract to its membership so many of the lively and influential undergraduates of the time was due almost entirely to Coupland's enthusiasm and energy, and not least to the high regard in which he was held in imperial circles both at home and overseas.'

And what remains now of all their work?

As I have put it in verse:

> They all served Church or State in their day
> Who now are here, shrouded in surplices
> As once they were who now are ghosts, alive
> Only in the dedicated mind.
> November sunlight flickers across the aisle,
> Falls upon stall and altar, whereon
> The candles shed their flame, and it is written:
> *The souls of the just are in the hand of God.**

---

* 'All Souls Day', in *Selected Poems*.

CHAPTER 24

Sir Keith Hancock

W.K. Hancock was one of the most original and distinctive historians of our time – a born writer, a first-class historian. An Australian Rhodes Scholar at Oxford, he had the advantage of a new perspective. His dominant idea was to be an interpreter of Australia to Britain, and of Britain to Australia. Thus he became a leading authority on Commonwealth Affairs, the Survey of which he wrote at periodic intervals, in 1937, 1940 and 1942. He belonged to the Empire and Commonwealth group at Oxford, centred upon All Souls. He observed the historic transition from colonial to Dominion status, equality within the Commonwealth; and within the Empire the ideal of trusteeship of native peoples not yet mature enough for self-government. (Nor were they – look at the evidences all round Africa, Nigeria, Uganda, Rwanda, Sudan, etc.)

Hancock began with Italian history, acquainting himself with the countryside in the most intimate way, sleeping in the open. I remember his enthusiasm for traditional folk customs, like the Palio at Siena, which gave colour to city life in better days. He wrote the first volume of a biography, Ricasoli and the Risorgimento in Tuscany. This he did not complete, he went on to so much else. He wrote a few other things on Italy: a couple of essays on Machiavelli, another on Ranalli, an independent observer of affairs; and an account of Italian *métayage*, which he studied on the ground. He was equally interested in economic and political history, sometimes professor of the one, sometimes of the other.

When Hancock left college to return to Australia he arranged with me, as Junior Fellow, to keep him in touch with what was going on over here. I have kept his letters. I recall sending on his fascinating study of Pitcairn Island to the *Nineteenth Century* for publication. Later, when his studies turned to Africa, he wrote an eloquent tribute to that splendid woman, Mary Kingsley, who dedicated her life, and eventually sacrificed it, to the Africans on the West Coast.

He moved about a good deal, between England and Australia, with a foray into South Africa. Professor at Adelaide, then at Birmingham; next back at Oxford, then London. During the Second War he worked hard all day in the Cabinet Office, under his All Souls colleague, Edward Bridges, engaged upon our war economy. At night he was fire-watching on the roof of St Paul's, throwing out fire-bombs from the leads. He had an overriding sense of civic duty, both to Britain and Australia, illuminating of both, sane and sensible, no complexes – let alone the aching inferiority complex of Patrick White. Though not a novelist – and no Nobel Prizeman, merely an historian – he was a better writer.

He might have made a wider impact if he had not moved about so much among various subjects and different places. He told Richard Pares that, if a door opened before him, he could not but go through it. And, with his ability and seductive charm, all doors were opened to him, especially government ones. People knew his good judgement, discretion and trustworthiness. This meant that he had influence where it mattered – with government, both in Britain and Australia. In Downing Street he was Supervisor of the wartime Civil Histories, covering many fields and different departments of state. A tremendous job, editing all the volumes and co-operating on some. For the last phase he went back to Australia to direct a Research School of the National University at Canberra.

I knew little of his work in these active jobs: to me he was first and last the writer, and thank goodness he kept at his writing all the time. He wrote an autobiography, *Country and Calling*, which I found less good, it was so reticent. What is the point of writing an autobiography if you are going to be so reserved? The son of an archdeacon of Melbourne, he was also highly ethical. He was married to a neurasthenic valetudinarian, whom we were not invited to meet. That may have helped to shut him up within himself – though a friendly man – and of course to concentrate on work.

As with any original writer one can see the kind of man he was from his work – there is no reticence there, he puts himself into it. His pieces on Machiavelli reveal Hancock's principles as a man and his practice as an historian. He rightly saw Machiavelli in the context of the Renaissance, when the struggle for power between states was absolute, and – as Burckhardt perceived – illegitimacy was its characteristic mark in Italy. Writing in the 1930s, Hancock noted, 'and the same tendency has appeared today in large areas of continental Europe'.

Familiar with Mussolini's Italy, he observed on returning to England that 'the air was thick' with ethical and juristic discussion. Confusion would be a better word, for we were fatally bemused in that decade. Hancock himself was not taken in by illusionists on the Left, who thought that pacific ideals were enough for dealing with Hitler and Mussolini, or with illusionists of the Right who thought that giving way to them would buy them off on reasonable terms.

Hancock perceived that 'the historian's judgement is similar to that of the statesman'. The statesman's first principle must be to safeguard the interest of his own country; but his work does not stop there: he must work to reconcile that with the interests of others, as far as possible with the general interest. This had been the sheet-anchor of England's success against the aggressive ascendancies of Philip II, Louis XIV, Napoleon, and the German Empire before 1914. If followed consistently it would have given security against Hitler's Germany, let alone Mussolini's Italy.

Hancock did not pursue this line of thought deeply enough. He should have seen that some states are aggressive by nature, their internal constitution dictates a policy not reconcilable with others. The leaders of pre-1914 Germany thought of external military advance as the alternative to internal social progress, possible social revolution. The alternative was implicit in

177

Mussolini's Italy, directing the gaze of the Italians to Mediterranean Empire, *Mare Nostro*.

Hitler and Mussolini recognised no law and morality above their own country's national power, no keeping of faith either. 'Law and morality' are Hancock's terms, the conventional ones: I have always preferred to think in terms of Interest, and the overriding need to reconcile the particular with the general interest. Apart even from questions of law and morality, keeping one's word, etc., Hitler and Mussolini were fundamentally uneducated. If they had been more educated they would have been more dangerous – but then, perhaps, they would not have tried it on, or do what they did.

From the first Hancock wrote that 'understanding the concrete facts of particular situations is the first task of sound historical judgement, as it is the first task of cool statesmanship. It is sometimes called a sense of reality.' Well, of course – but how few people have it!

The heavyweight economic historian, the sombre Sombart, wrote, 'No theory, no history.' Typically German. Equally German is the theme of their eminent political theorist, Meinecke – I remember Hancock reading his *Staats-Räson* at All Souls: 'The state, it seems, must *sündigen*' (i.e. do wrong). Hitler subscribed to that, and acted on it throughout. It was ultimately not a good idea, if successful in the short term – safer to act in accord with the general interest.

In writing history facts are primary, and, without subjecting them to any thesis, they add up and point in the direction in which things are going. Hancock had no difficulty in demolishing the absurd theory of Professor Hicks (whom I had defeated for the Fellowship at All Souls): 'Economic history is just the applied economics of earlier ages.' The great Marshall, mentor of the new subject, knew better. 'To explain the economic leadership of England he invoked geography, with a particularly keen eye to its influence upon transport. He invoked war, particularly those wars from which England held aloof. He invoked technology, science, education, politics, morals, religion, and national temperament.'

178

In short, 'economic theory is by itself an insufficient guide to economic fact'. Even to achieve a satisfactory theory 'it is only by the most rigorous abstraction that the organon can be made truly universal; but by the same abstraction it becomes remote from specific historical situations'.

Hicks was a mathematical economist whose forecast of the dollar was completely falsified. Myself, I have always held that economics is a practical subject, dealing with the actualities of the real world, not a branch of abstract mathematics. And we have evidences of how wrong their forecasts can be, even apart from the multiple confusion of their advice. Plain factual common sense, like Adam Smith's or Walter Bagehot's, is more reliable.

Already in 1930 with his book, *Australia*, Hancock had written the best book ever to be produced on the subject. Though forgotten today, it may be considered a classic portrait, up to 1930 – and can any demotic society have been bettered since? Keith was in love with his own strange country, history, geography, ecology, anthropology, landscapes, everything. The book fascinated me. What a country! A whole continent, empty and dried up at the centre, occupied and alive only along the incredibly drawn-out rim. The highly civilised author loved the life of the bush, camping out, swimming in the rivers (not on Bondi Beach). I was electrified when he told me that once, when swimming, a large snake swam across his chest.

> And the snake in hiding feels the sunlight's finger,
> The snake, the fang of summer, beauty's double meaning,
> Shifts his slow coils and feels his springtime hunger.

Happily there was none of the boring headache about being colonial:

> Such savage and scarlet as no green hills dare
> Springs in that waste, some spirit which escapes
> The learned doubt, the chatter of cultured apes
> Which is called civilisation over there.

179

Hancock was inspired by the contrasts and the continuities between the old country and the new – which, underneath the newcomers, was so much older. He was in love with both, as I was with Cornwall and England cheek-by-jowl – only his were many thousands of miles apart, in those days before air travel. It was a creative act to bring them together in his mind.

When my friend Lord De L'Isle went as Governor-General I gave him Hancock's book as introduction and guide. To his wife I gave my Australian friend Guy Howarth's *Penguin Book of Modern Australian Verse*. I greatly admired the work of their best poet, Judith Wright, and never forgot the drama of her killing a very poisonous snake:

> O beat him into the ground.
> O strike him till he dies,
> Or else your life itself
> Drains through those colourless eyes.

She had her own lament for 'white Australians' treatment of the land itself. Eroded soils, the destruction of forests and wild life.' She travelled all round the vast country, 'observing the havoc we had caused'.

Hancock followed up his book with further essays on England and Australia, the relations between the two. 'In establishing a complete political democracy England followed slowly in the wake of Australia. Five of the six Australian Colonies had a democratic suffrage as early as the fifties of the last century. The principle of payment of MPs was established in Victoria in 1878; British democracy had to fight for it for another generation. The women of South Australia were granted the vote in 1895; English women did not win it until after the 1914–18 War.'

There were other delightful amenities in which the old country was to follow: state intervention in industry, the promotion of Trade Union power, though we have not yet achieved the bonus of compulsory voting. All this should have soothed sore heads about the Pommies. Keith was a very tactful man.

*

His next venture was into the troubled waters of South Africa. He was invited to write the official biography of Smuts. He spent several years over this big task, producing two volumes, in 1962 and 1968. He kept up his contacts with All Souls, where I met him after the appearance of the first volume. Oddly enough, I did not fall for this – it was my failing, I suspect, not his.

Or did Hancock's cool reticence fail to put across what a great man Smuts was? After a brilliant career at Cambridge he went back to the Transvaal to become the youngest member of old President Kruger's government. Knowing the resources Britain could command, he opposed the determination of Kruger's followers, with their Bible and back-veldt mentality, to fight Britain. Defeated over this, he loyally followed his people, becoming one of their brilliant cavalry commanders, raiding far and wide, and very hard to catch.

The Boers lost the war, but won the peace. By compromising with the Boers, the Liberal government in Britain won the aid and support of South Africa in the cruel testing time of the two great German Wars. Smuts fought for Britain in the first. In the second he gave counsel and strategic advice of the utmost value to Churchill. When Smuts, with his British following, lost power the pure Boer spirit took over with its fetish of Apartheid. An historian may observe that, if Britain had maintained her ascendancy, there would never have been Apartheid.

One saw the kind of man Smuts was when he came to us at All Souls: tall, erect military bearing, those steel-grey eyes, an Olympian figure, not very approachable, as people found (unlike the very human Botha). Had Hancock perhaps found that?

In those grand days one met them all on our hearth: Smuts and the unimpressive Herzog, his rival; brilliant Jan Hofmeyr, Smuts's intended heir who, alas, died young; Patrick Duncan, the Governor-General; Sir Abe Bailey, the philanthropic millionaire who funded Lionel Curtis's brain-child, Chatham House, the Royal Institute of International Affairs, which provided a home for Arnold Toynbee and a rest-house for other historians. Hancock was involved in its work, and produced three of its Surveys. But his special interest was in the concept of 'Commonwealth', going right back to its roots in mid-Tudor days, with its widening, yet useful, connotations for our time. I remember his enthusiasm for those early Tudor writers, Starkey, Sir Thomas Smith, and especially John Hales, with his *Discourse of the Common Weal of this Realm of England.*

'When the framers of our federal constitution decided that Australia was to be a *Commonwealth*, they vindicated the imperishable future of a word which already, centuries earlier, had stirred the imagination of our ancestors.' Thus Hancock wrote, who had imagination as well as scholarship. Does the word stir any imagination today? Probably not – so much the worse for the demotic monochrome, with its attendant squalors, of an Americanised world. Hancock belonged to that Commonwealth group at Oxford, which served the world well in its time and also, we may say, stood for more civilised values and standards.

For the last phase of his life Hancock went back to serve Australia, as Director of the Research School of Social Studies at the National University at Canberra. Something like the Institute of Advanced Study at Princeton, which was founded on the model of All Souls. Hancock was well equipped to give it direction and to set standards. Of his work there I know only his last remarkable book, *Discovering Monaco*, 1972. This was a survey of a section of upland country, on the south-east border of New South Wales, quite exceptional as having surplus rainfall and water resources in the arid continent. Hancock's Survey was exceptional too, in the astonishing detail and depth of his exploration – into everything; we may take his penetration and perception for granted. Though he published two more collections of essays, including *Perspectives in History*, 1982, we may close with that investigation into, and evocation of, his beloved country, for I know nothing else quite like it for its combination of science and poetry.

CHAPTER 25

Sir Michael Howard

Sir Michael Howard is our foremost military historian, one of the finest writers on strategy and the history of war that this country has produced. Here we are concerned only with his contributions to history.

From Christ Church he came in for our Prize Fellowship examination at All Souls. I was in favour of his election, but was defeated by Warden Sparrow, who favoured a more flowery, literary candidate, who in the whole course of his life surprisingly wrote nothing. Michael wrote concisely, too briefly; but the quality was there. Later, he matured into one of the best of writers as such.

For his first work he wrote the History of the Coldstream Guards, 1920–46, to which Sparrow lent his name, though Michael did practically all the work. This was followed by a volume of Wellingtonian Studies, and then a masterpiece, *The Franco-Prussian War* of 1870–71. I know no account of a war to surpass it, in description and narration, analysis and judgement. It has its living personal side. It was a ghastly experience for France – in one sense dominating the French consciousness up to 1914, with the ever-present ache of the loss of Alsace-Lorraine.

And the lesson it brings home as to human foolery in high places! With the Empress Eugénie pushing the ailing Napoleon III into war when France was unprepared – '*Il faut en finir*'! She well deserved her place in the tradition of Marie Antoinette, and other *femmes fatales*, like Henrietta Maria or the Tsar Nicholas II's wife.

Howard followed this with a series of remarkable books on

strategy, with which we are not concerned, even if I understood the subject. Perhaps, however, I may say that throughout the period of the Cold War – the West confronting Soviet Russia – I followed his judgement of the situation with most respect. He understood the complexities of the nuclear balance of power, and expounded them as no other writer.

When he succeeded to the Chichele Chair of Military History at All Souls in 1968 – which he held until 1980 – the title was changed to that of the History of War. This suited him, for he produced notable volumes on its nature, and various aspects of the subject: *War in European History, The Causes of War, War and the Liberal Conscience*.

What a corrective these were of the illusions so many entertained, in reaction to the appalling experience, the blood-drain of 1914–18. I recall the simple statement of that man of good judgement, C.R. Attlee, in reply to the pacifist illusions so strong on the Left, that pacifism wasn't practical politics, however desirable. The world isn't made like that, neither that of humans, nor of Nature 'red in tooth and claw'.

This leads on to Howard's authoritative treatment of Clausewitz, the classic philosopher of war (a German, of course), so much and so easily misunderstood. Fortunately, not our subject here. Howard explains him for us, once and for all.

Perhaps I may put an historical point at issue. The leading German historian of the two great wars of 1914–18 and 1939–45, Fritz Fischer, regards them as two waves in the Thirty Years War of our time. He sees them as continuous, arising out of the same causes and dispositions, the race of Germany to achieve world power.

In a recent lecture Howard questions the continuity and emphasises the differences. There was of course a difference between the German military hierarchy of pre-1914, which was at least a part of European civilisation, and the barbarism of Nazi Germany – though the generals backed Hitler's rearmament and swore the oath of fealty to him as Führer in Frederick the Great's church at Potsdam.

The real point here is not any difference of appearances but the continuity of objectives. Hitler's onslaught on Russia for

Lebensraum and the control of Eastern Europe is entirely continuous with Germany's Eastern objective in 1914–18. This is only too clear from their Treaty of Brest-Litovsk in 1917, by which Germany took all Eastern Europe right up to the threshold of St Petersburg.

We need no further argument: the *core* of the matter was continuous. When an official of the German Foreign Office protested at the unfortunate effect this would have on foreign opinion (particularly with the idealistic President Wilson), Ludendorff replied that he needed all that Baltic area to manoeuvre his left wing in the next war! Note, Ludendorff was Hitler's colleague in his *Putsch* in Munich in 1923.

I am myself in complete agreement with Fritz Fischer.

I knew well the first holder of the chair of Military History, Spenser Wilkinson. He was a reputable historian, though his real importance was in practical affairs. He was the brother-in-law of Sir Eyre Crowe, permanent head of our Foreign Office, who had a German wife and was fully cognisant of affairs in Germany, the Kaiser's ambivalent, neurotic character and his Byzantine entourage, etc.

Wilkinson served this country well in his constant propaganda for a general staff, following Germany, for both Army and Navy. He wrote two books, in addition to incessant articles in the *Morning Post: The Brain of an Army*, and *The Brain of the Navy*. Fortunately he was in time with his campaign, before the challenge matured in 1914.

He wrote two history books, *The French Army before Napoleon*, and *The Rise of General Bonaparte*. When I came to All Souls, still a youth, he was in retirement, a slightly lubricious, bearded veteran in spats. I found him a sentimental bore, and read none of his books. He had a notorious story about being arrested as a spy in Cracow, which took up to half an hour in the telling. He never succeeded in telling it to me.

He was followed by a less competent successor, but more genial personality, General Sir Ernest Swinton. He was reputed to have had a hand in the official History of the Russo-Japanese War, but was known to us as the author of a best-selling volume of Kiplingesque short stories. The author was Ole-Luk-Oie, which had the appeal of mystery, for he would never tell where it came from or what it meant. Apparently it is Danish, and means Shut-Eye. Where can we have got it from?

He was a sapper, a talented technician who had a great part in the invention of the tank, working out its military use, tactical employment, etc. This had Churchill's support from the Admiralty until he was sacked after the Dardanelles fiasco, but it was constantly held up by lack of imagination in the Army authorities. When eventually employed in the battle of Cambrai in November 1917, it was used on an inadequate scale with no idea of its potential.

This left Swinton an embittered man with a complex. Ironically, tragically, his daughter was knocked down and killed by a tank outside their home in Oxford. I found the old boy rather a dear, but was youthfully surprised by his mess-room habit of telling the same story over and over. He cannot have read Swift's warning in 'Resolutions for when I come to be Old'.

Cyril Falls was a person of charm, distinction, even elegance of style as man and as writer. A loyal Ulsterman, he wrote the story of his own regiment, the 36th (Ulster Division) in which he had served. Michael Howard says that it contains 'some of the finest descriptions of conditions on the Western Front to be found anywhere in the history of the War'.

He was a very proficient full-time writer, contributing three volumes to the history of that war: on the Egyptian and Palestine Campaign, on that in Macedonia, and on the struggle on the Western Front in the touch-and-go year 1917. In 1930 he followed with *War Books*, in which he considered the popular anti-war books of the time in the proper historical context, rationally as against their emotional appeal. During all these years he was the *Times* military correspondent, adding to it a column in the *Illustrated London News*.

25. Sir Michael Howard

He came to us as professor for all too short a time, 1946–53. As such he wrote a book on *Elizabeth I's Irish Wars*, where he knew the topography on his own home ground. Following upon it, I suggested that he write for Odham's Press, which I was advising, a biography of *Mountjoy: Elizabethan General*. This was a congenial subject, which Cyril made the most of. Mountjoy was the handsome young fellow of the Blount family – a diverse and questionable lot – a favourite of the Queen, who appointed him to clear up the mess which Essex had made in Ireland, instead of quelling the O'Neil's resistance in Ulster. It took Mountjoy two or three years to complete the job, for he was distracted by a Spanish incursion in force in the South. Mountjoy's long liaison with Essex's beautiful sister, the wife of Lord Rich, was recognised by society, until Mountjoy married the lady, when social humbug made a scandal of it. All this appealed to Cyril, who had a soldierly gallantry for the fair sex.

He ended his career with an admirably concise history of the *First World War*. This was after his retirement from college, from which I missed him greatly, for he had become a close friend and ally.

His successor as professor was an ordinary teaching don from another college, who shall be nameless, though his tenure of the chair was hardly blameless. As Michael Howard said of it, he sat in it for fifteen years and did nothing. He took a pompous interest in our wine-cellar – he affected a judicious palate – and enjoyed the tenancy of one of our houses at historic Stanton Harcourt.

It took Michael to restore the repute of the chair, though I never understood why he thought it worth while to vacate it for the chores of the Regius Professorship. The United States proved a more strategic post in our day and time.

187

CHAPTER 26

Denis Mack Smith

Denis Mack Smith is our leading historian of modern Italy, recognised as such in Italy itself, in spite of party prejudices, for the excellence of his work. There he is thought of as a man of the Left, for his sympathies are certainly not with Mussolini and Fascism. We shall probably be not far wrong in thinking of him as in the mainstream of European Liberal thought, in its disillusioned contemporary inflexion.

What makes it difficult to place him is his care to be as impartial as possible throughout his work, in the minefield of modern Italy. He succeeds without being direly impersonal: he is not afraid of saying what he thinks when occasion demands.

Characteristic of his work is the thoroughness of his research, his mastery of the sources of every kind, printed and manuscript, archives as well as newspapers. Then there is the clarity with which all is set out.

A Cambridge man, Mack Smith began with a book on Cavour and Garibaldi in the year 1860. One notices at once the contrast with the lyrical enthusiasm for Garibaldi and the Risorgimento of Trevelyan, then leader in this field. No enthusiasm, let alone lyricism in Mack Smith. All is at a prose level, at a cool even temperature, and all the more trustworthy. It is not only a difference of personality, and of gifts, but it represents a difference of generation. We have none of the idealism, the hopes and illusions of the Victorians. We have been through too much. The tragic experience of the twentieth century has taught us the facts of life, truths about mankind – not least in regard to Italy.

Mack Smith followed with a biography of Garibaldi, whom the Victorians idolised. Here he is treated with respect, but not made an idol of. There succeeded several volumes which I have read in, but not all through. Dr Johnson was a dipper, and said to someone who inquired, 'Do *you* read books all through?' Well, I almost invariably do, but have not read *Italy: a Modern History*, in either original or enlarged edition; or the two volumes on Medieval and Modern Sicily; or that on Victor Emmanuel, Cavour and the Risorgimento.

All Souls made Denis a Research Fellow, which freed him to concentrate on writing. Brought over from Cambridge, he was an ornament to the Oxford scene, without taking much part in it. A reserved and reticent man, he concentrated on writing, as I did. On this we were at one, unlike prominent actors such as A.J.P. Taylor, and we became friends.

Though Denis was never forthcoming, I could occasionally put a query and learn something. He thought, for instance, that if Cavour had lived he might have tackled effectively the problem of the South – the enduring sore in an Italy united, and dominated, by the North. But this foremost Italian statesman was virtually killed by his doctors, who bled him to death.

A later book, *Italy and its Monarchy*, is characteristically aware of the problems that press up on all sides upon the actors on the human stage – by birth or choice or election – and the difficulty of getting anything right in politics. For instance, we learn that both Garibaldi and Mazzini died disillusioned men: for all that the unification of Italy had been achieved, it had not worked out in the way they envisaged, or answered their hopes. (Are anybody's in politics? For all that they wrought, Cromwell, and even Lenin, died in some disillusion with it.)

'The dynasty of Savoy had a history that was as much French as Italian, and had been slow to accept the idea of unifying the peninsula.' Both Victor Emmanuel I and Cavour spoke French and disliked having to speak Italian. Mazzini, who kept the ideal of a united Italy alive more than anyone, wanted a democratic republic. An impossible dream on all counts.

'The monarchy had a central role in the story of how Italy developed into a modern nation state.' I do not think that Denis has any bias in favour of monarchs, and he regards Italy's four kings as having no qualities that raised them above the ranks of ordinary people. That is not saying much for them. Then he adds justly, 'And yet all of them confronted political problems that would have severely tested people of greater intelligence and force of character.'

We come to the central figure, and development, in Italy's history in our time, Mussolini and Fascism, to which Denis devoted two books: *Mussolini's Roman Empire*, and a full-length biography of the creator of Fascism and of his short-lived empire.

It is extraordinarily difficult for any Englishman – and Denis is very English – to do justice to the personality and career of Mussolini. For he represented all that the English most dislike and despise: the boasting and *braggadocio*, the vanity and posturings, the operatics, not to mention the gangsterism, elements of criminality, the beatings-up and murders. Yet they underestimated his intelligence, for underneath all this he *was* intelligent, a skilled politician and effective propagandist. Mack Smith admits the skill with which he stayed in power for twenty years, and held in thrall a volatile, changeable, if childish, people.

How did he get there, from small, improbable beginnings?

I should say, shortly, by the idiocy of Italian Liberal politicians, who frustrated and manoeuvred each other off the stage, left it wide open for someone with more will-power to occupy it. They could not pull together to keep the enemy out, who had taken their measure – as they had not taken his. They deserved what they got – as did the infantile People who gave him their support, and eventually their lives.

Not all of them were duped. I remember in Rome waiting in the piazza to hear him speak, comfortably ensconced in a doorway reading Machiavelli's *The Prince* while I waited. This was in 1938, after the success of the Abyssinian adventure, when the British – who played their hand so badly and were defeated by him – were unpopular in Italy. Out upon the balcony of the Palazzo Venezia came the familiar figure – short, squat, heavy-jowled, darkly shaven like a convict. His voice oddly reminded me of George Lansbury's, hoarse with outdoor speaking. But the gestures were those of an artist, with which he punctuated his clichés about '*nostra volunta è nostra fede*'.

The Roman crowd were not enthusiastic. I noticed the scepticism of an old, sophisticated people. One or two near me, recognising me as English, smiled in a friendly way and more or less gave me a wink. I registered the contrast with Germany, where people with no sense of humour sopped up the beliefs preached to them by Hitler.

And indeed, Margarita Sarfatti told me that Mussolini for himself didn't like the Germans. She was the intelligent Milanese Jewess who had been an early patron and then his mistress, until pushed out by envious daughter, Edda Ciano, for the younger Clara Petacci, who shared his fate. These belonged to the pro-Hitler bunch, who pushed him into that embrace, when the Sarfatti's sympathies were Anglo-American.

Then why did Mussolini take the wrong turning?

Hugh Dalton, very much in touch with foreign affairs, who appreciated Mussolini's intelligence from a long talk with him, gives us the answer. It was simply that Hitler had more to offer him than Britain and France could. If one looks at the map in Mack Smith's book one sees the obvious lure. There are Nice (Nizza) and Savoy, which Napoleon III had exacted for his services; there is Corsica, which had belonged to Genoa, almost in sight of the Italian mainland. Then, half-way to Africa, Malta, only a step to Tunisia with its large Italian population – and onwards to the further spaces of Africa, the already conquered Ethiopia, of which Victor Emmanuel III was proclaimed Emperor.

In short, Mussolini was tempted, and he fell. He had made the swap from his early socialism to nationalism, as our Oman had observed in Milan in 1922, while the bourgeoisie opted for Mussolini and his Fascists, to keep down the Communists. From his extreme nationalist stance to forward imperialism lay in the logic of history for Mussolini. Hence the mistake of lining up with Hitler in 1940 against Britain and France.

Mack Smith tells us that Italy did not expect defeat. This is surprising to an English reader. However, politicians have to be optimistic, it is their vocational disease – as de Gaulle says, *'Pour agir il faut espérer.'* If one has no hope one doesn't join in absurd human affairs. In Italy one outpost had a longer view: the Vatican realised that, behind Britain and France, there remained the United States.

All the same, we may reflect that, if Mussolini had not joined hands with Hitler, he would not have been able to renew the First German War from a far more advantageous strategical position.

In 1994 Mack Smith published his most mature, and possibly most difficult, work, his biography of *Mazzini*. For the research itself was daunting: Denis groaned to me about the ten thousand letters published and the hundred volumes of the collected works. Nevertheless he accomplished it with his usual mastery, and more than his usual sympathy in dealing with monarchs.

In fact a figure emerged rather different from that to which we were accustomed. We recognised the idealist, but found that Mazzini was more of a practical politician than we had supposed. For all his republicanism, his illusions about democracy, and his hopes of a spontaneous impulse of the Italian people towards unity, Mazzini was prepared to co-operate with the Savoy monarchy in default of it.

Marx was contemptuous of Mazzini as he was of almost everybody. Mazzini, the great opponent of the Temporal power of the Papacy, was yet a Christian as well as an idealist. In spite of Marx's harsh realism (and his own optimistic illusions about the working class and proletarian revolution), it remains evident that some element of idealism is necessary to hold society together – not least obviously in Italy itself.

From this point of view Denis shows no sympathy with the necessary role of the Church. This gave me the thought to tease him with the subject of a Pope for his next biography – say, the liberal-minded Leo XIII. Denis had already teased me, when I made the identification of Emilia Bassano, Mrs Lanier, as Shakespeare's young mistress. He surprised me by surfacing for once with, 'I couldn't care less who Shakespeare's Dark Lady was.' I replied, 'If you had discovered something new in the life of Michelangelo, I should be the first person to be interested.'

For, of course, historians ought always *to want to know*, it is their duty to find out.

CHAPTER 27

Barbara Tuchman

Marooned on my headland in Cornwall, I have not Barbara Tuchman's works conveniently to hand. In any case I am not in a position to survey her work as a whole. It covers such a wide span and deals with subjects which are not mine. *A Distant Mirror: The Calamitous Fourteenth Century* was her own favourite. That was the period of the Black Death, which exterminated a third of Europe's population and broke the spirit and ideals of the early Middle Ages – as ours have been in our own calamitous century. It was exceptional for a modern historian to manage a masterly medieval performance. More characteristic of her work are her books on America's entry into the two world wars; *The Zimmerman Telegram*; Jewish History and the recreation of Israel; US Relations with China.

Still, Miss Tuchman gave us a whole volume reviewing her past work, and it so happens that in her volume, *Practising History*, she considers the problems involved in writing history, along with her own experience, and with unwonted candour. This is characteristically American of her, though she has a trenchant forthrightness, an absolute honesty all her own. English historians are more cagey, and shrink from exposing themselves. I have several times been asked to set down what I think about my craft, and my own practice in writing history. In my unregenerate earlier days I ventured to write a book on only one aspect of the subject, *The Use of History*. But it is the work, the research, in and for itself, that interests me, inspires me and – Barbara Tuchman would add – the writing it up. She regarded that as more important, and gave short shrift to minds not qualified to judge.

Here I not only agree with her, but *feel along with her* as she writes, in the way that I do, strangely enough, in reading Berenson about landscape and art, Santayana or Wittgenstein about philosophy. It happens too that I was lucky enough to know her, and I hope that I can give some idea of her personality and how it enters into her work. She was the granddaughter of Henry Morgenthau, senior, who was the effective backer of Woodrow Wilson for President; and niece of Henry Morgenthau, junior, who was President Franklin Roosevelt's closest ally in his Cabinet.

This had the result of Tuchman's approach to history being *governmental*, with a deep sense of responsibility and the necessity, above all, for good judgement. In these crucial respects she cannot be faulted: this is why I respect her so much – as against the crying defect of, say, A.J.P. Taylor's light-headed irresponsibility and lack of judgement. In history, as in politics, *judgement* is fundamental, a prime necessity. Among American historians the famous, and populist, historian Charles Beard did not have it. Thus he offers a pretty parallel to our TV historian, Taylor. A great historian, Samuel Eliot Morison, called Beard to order, and put paid to him, in his treatment, 'The Shaving of a Beard'.

Barbara Tuchman was as courageous as she was outspoken, and did not hesitate to reveal the secrets of our trade, or what she thought about the inexpert in it, as against polite English disingenuousness. This did not make her popular in the profession – though they would have done better to sit down and learn from her. She had the advantage of an upper-class education and outlook, of liberal principles and a wide culture – rather European in its bearings, very well read in English literature. I add two notably Jewish characteristics, her generosity and public-spiritedness.

Like Allan Nevins she served her apprenticeship in journalism, and this taught her how to write – the hard way, for on the whole, the older generation of American journalists wrote better than run-of-the-mill academics, glued to the Ph.D. She learned that selection is the clue to making a book of it, not a Ph.D. thesis. 'Selection is the task of distinguishing the significant from the insignificant. It must be honest – that is, true to the circumstances; and fair – that is truly representative.'

This speaks for me. It is surprising how often American historians show no idea of what is significant, and what is insignificant. They are apt to think bigger is better – when it usually is not. My friend Gordon Ray, in writing his biography of Thackeray, began with the dimensions of the ship in which Thackeray's parents went to India! What is the point of that? Carl van Doren, in his thousand-page biography of Benjamin Franklin, claimed that he had 'pared it to the bone'. He evidently couldn't tell a bone when he saw one. As for the thousand-page biographies à la Mr Manchester of Presidents like Kennedy, or simply of Presidential campaigns à la White, they sicken a civilised reader. Manchester goes all round the universe recording what everyone was doing when he heard the news of Kennedy's assassination. What is the significance of such items? One doesn't want to be told every time the President goes to the lavatory.

To Miss Tuchman each detail had to be significant, or she ruthlessly sacrificed it, even when it appealed to her. She was a self-conscious artist, very sharply aware of what was relevant and what was not. She exemplified the good standards of earlier Americans, Parkman and Prescott, or, for that matter, of Franklin or Jefferson, who wrote briefly and concisely.

Nor was she afraid to take offending British historians to task. Here is the verbose Professor Denis Brogan. In his *'France under the Republic* for example, one can count thirty names to a page, all faceless'. Even Sir Michael Howard, who was too constricted when young, is exposed for such a sentence in his book on the Franco-Prussian war: 'The Emperor put Failly's 5th Corps under his command and on 5th August while the division of 1st Corps concentrated around Froeschwiller and Felix Donay packed off Conseil Dumesnil's division from 7th Corps by train from Belfort, MacMahon summoned Failly', etc. She concludes: 'I did not get a picture from it of the Battle of Froeschwiller but only how *not* to describe a battle.' Perhaps this is a bit hard on our best military historian today.

Then she has a salutary warning about knowing when to stop. 'One must stop *before* one has finished, otherwise one will never stop and never finish.' There is always something more to put in, and one learns from experience to resist the temptation to hold up the work to put it in. After all, there is another day – perhaps another book, as I have found with my Shakespeare research. As we have seen, my friend Pares came up with three hundred thousand words of shapeless primary research, out of which Clark and Namier excavated two possible books and a couple of articles. McFarlane, our best authority on fifteenth century England, never could bring his research to a stop, but left it for his devout pupils to produce it in book form. It took Arnold Toynbee twelve volumes of his *Study of History* before he came to a stop. Absurd – all that he had to say was better said in the two-volume abridgement of his work by others.

On the positive side Miss Tuchman urges what may be a counsel of perfection: you should be 'in love with your subject'. I don't think that Pares was – though he made himself the master of it, he was too *désabusé* with it. Here again she speaks for me. I can honestly claim that I have been 'in love' with Cornwall all my life – though it may be obvious enough in my books and poems. Similarly with the Elizabethan age and with William Shakespeare. It may be sentimental to say so, but that love has kept me going, into my tenth decade. Well, Ranke went on writing history into his nineties.

Barbara quotes him as preferring the truth about a period as more romantic than the romances – for example, of Walter Scott, let alone of lesser historical novelists. *Ich auch.* I suspect that this is why I don't really like historical novels – especially about periods and subjects with which one is more familiar oneself. With Ranke, I find the truth more fascinating. As I have said, notably about Shakespeare – the truth, the facts about him and his work, when one finds them out, are immeasurably more interesting than conjectures, of minds not up to the level of the subject or not qualified by knowledge to hold an opinion. Let alone the sheer dottiness that proliferates in a demotic age with no standards. Hers were elect standards – those which alone are worth consideration.

She held that narrative history had a great advantage. 'As a form, narrative has an inherent validity because it is the key to the problem of causation. Events do not happen in categories – economic, intellectual, military – they happen in sequence.' I add to this a perhaps unexpected consideration – narrative history is both more flexible and more subtle. It has the qualities of life, which after all is the material of history. In our time there has been a fashion for analytical history, for approximating it to sociology, answering questions put to it. However the questions vary with the questioners and with the fashions, the answers then are superseded, in fact they go out of fashion very quickly. There is a sense in which Thucydides is not superseded, and Herodotus is never out of fashion.

Perhaps we may venture to say that much the same holds good for Plutarch. Again I am at one with Miss Tuchman in her view of 'Biography as a Prism of History'. She says, 'Unhappily, biography has lately been overtaken by a school that has abandoned the selective in favour of the all-inclusive. I think this development is part of the anti-excellence spirit of our time that insists on the equality of everything, and is thus reduced to the theory that all facts are of equal value and that the biographer or historian should not presume to exercise judgement.' On this attitude she comes down trenchantly: 'To that I can only say, if he cannot exercise judgement he should not be in the business.' I admire the forthrightness of this as much as its common sense.

There is a silly cliché going the rounds today, without thought, that one should not be 'judgemental'. How fatuous! – when it is the business of the critic to judge why Andrew Wyeth is a better artist that Jackson Pollock, or Robert Frost a better poet than Allan Ginsburg. I know why we are told not to be 'judgemental' – Barbara Tuchman was perceptive enough to see that this was part of the ploy to reduce all to the same level, not to judge the third-rate for what they are.

She thought that history was by way of taking the place of the novel. She may be right about this, at any rate in the confusion as to the nature of the novel. Here I am not sure, for is it not the character of the novel to be more diverse, more unrestricted and comprehensive than any other genre? One feature of today does strike me as odd, perhaps significant: *everybody*, qualified or unqualified, seems to be writing about the past, now that the present is so uncongenial. Up to the post-war dissolution of Empire there was active British enterprise all round the globe. Now people are writing about it rather than acting. Contrast the activism of the Victorian age – true, they wrote it up as well as acted it. Today Britain is a museum.

Though a stoic, Tuchman was horrified by the twentieth century reversion to barbarism – the 'Terrible Century' as Churchill called it. As an historian she diagnosed the turning-point as having been the First German War, 1914–18. Before that, the nineteenth century belief in continuing progress and expanding liberty had prevailed. Britain largely believed in this and, as the American critic, Paul Fussell, perceived, was psychologically unprepared for the horrors released by it.

She had no difficulty equally in perceiving who were responsible for the reversion. She knew that, though stories of German atrocities in Belgium during the First War were exaggerated, they had taken place. A quarter of Louvain, with its ancient library, *had* been burnt down *in terrorem*. I was in Louvain not long after. A woman said to me that there had been no excuse, the Germans had not been fired on: '*tout le monde avait peur*.' Nurse Cavell, that brave Cornish woman, *has* been shot by them for getting what soldiers she could away into safety. She faced the firing squad unflinching, having regarded the saving of life but simple human duty.

The historian recognises that this is continuous – as the aims of German policy were – with the unimaginable horrors perpetrated in their Second War: the Final Solution, the extermination of Europe's Jews, six million human lives. 'The immensity of the task suggests the numbers of Germans involved in it: lawyers to draw up the decrees, civil servants to administer them, virtually the whole of the SS to carry out the program, police and certain sections of the Army to assist them, trainmen and truck-drivers to transport the victims, clerks to keep the statistics, bank tellers to tabulate gold teeth and wedding rings salvaged from the millions of corpses – not to mention the fortunate citizens who received Jewish property, businesses, and belongings.'

It may be unimaginable to us today, but it took place in our lifetime, and it is a German quality to be methodical and keep the records scrupulously for all to read. It has been usual to put it all down to the Nazis, the SS and their agents, and to exonerate the *Wehrmacht* – the German Army with its 'honourable' tradition. But quite recently uncovered records have shown that the *Wehrmacht* was active in the Holocaust as well, if not to the same extent.

Sir Michael Howard uses the polite term 'cultural heterogeneity' for the German record. It is the duty of historians to describe things truthfully, *wie es eigentlich gescheht*, as it actually happens, in Ranke's words. It is therefore more truthful, and unavoidable, for the historian, to diagnose and to judge this as the reversion to barbarism – which it released and set going in this terrible century.

It is sometimes argued that Stalin's Russia was no better – as if that were any excuse. Historians know that Russia does not yet qualify as part of Western civilisation: she never went through the fundamental experiences of the West – the Renaissance, the Reformation, the social and political gains of the French Revolution. To those we might add the experience of Rome. Germany, however, has long been part of Western civilisation, regarded by some as its centre (not by me). And, after all, this was the *twentieth* century, not the seventeenth with its barbarous Thirty Years War. There really is no exoneration. Part of the trouble with easy-going Britain in regard to it all was that her people could not imagine that it could happen.

Continentals knew better. The neighbouring Swiss, Romain Rolland, could hear the bullying note, the threat, before 1914 in Strauss's music – one can certainly hear it in *Ein Heldenleben*: 'Aha! Germany the All-Powerful, *der Allermächte*, will not keep her balance for long!' More than unbalance was indicated, to

those capable of reading the signs. They were all to be read in
Mein Kampf – but few are capable of reading with intelligence.

Barbara Tuchman was a woman of the Thirties, and could
read the signs, as I am a man of the Thirties. A liberal and a
democrat, she says that her 'heart was cracked politically' by the
defeat of the Spanish Republic in the Civil War – as mine was
cracked before, by Britain's fatal Election in 1931 and Hitler's
achievement of power eighteen months later. I *knew* he would
never let go – he had the German people with him to the end –
and told Adam von Trott, 'You may roll up the map of Europe.'
Our hopes were ended.

In contemplating all that has happened in our century –
wrecked as it was – Tuchman maintains her balance, her
historical sense of proportion. By family background and
conviction she was a Democrat. But her indictment of Nixon as
President does not rest on partisanship; it is all the more
convincing because she rests it on historical grounds. His
personal conduct of the Presidency undermined one of the three
main pillars of the Constitution, the division of power devised by
the Founding Fathers – Presidency, Congress, Supreme Court
and the rule of law. In this we may see Tuchman as not so much
a Democrat as a good Whig – like Burke.

We know that Nixon was so schizophrenic as to be almost two
separable persons. He hated the illusions, the hallucinations,
the humbug of the liberal establishment, the media and the
intelligentsia so much that it overbalanced his judgement, at
least in home affairs and dirty domestic politics. In world affairs
he did well. He was especially proud of breaking the log-jam of
US relations with China. It was a prime historic achievement,
and perhaps only he could have done it. The United States had
long been bemused, taken in, by American idealising of China.
Nixon was no idealist, but an earth-bound realist. He was
contemptuous of idealist humbug – like American illusions
about Britain's beneficent Commonwealth as 'imperialism',
when the real imperialism was that of Stalin's Russia. So Nixon
was a good friend of Britain, and we did not get Watergate out of

proportion – that kind of thing was to be expected of American party politicking.

I knew President Nixon, though only on the good side. He used to send me all his books. He read history. Because Jack Kennedy, with whom Nixon had an acute sense of rivalry, had a favourite historical work, my friend David Cecil's *Melbourne*, Nixon had to have his: Robert Blake's weightier *Disraeli*. Nixon was proud to be the first President to appoint two Jews to high office, Kissinger and Annenberg – though he did not think of that at the time, he said. (I wonder?) In his enforced retirement he took to writing history – though I suppose we might put him as historian in the class of Beaverbrook.

I kept an ear open to Nixon's dicta, which were revealing. Of Eisenhower: 'He was always the politician.' He, with the aid of the dreadful Dulles, certainly wrecked Britain's position in the Middle East over Suez. And Dulles afterwards said that we should have gone on, not given up! As a moderate determinist, not a complete fatalist, I suppose it was all rather inevitable. When I suggested that the United States should stand ready for the time when 'disarray' appeared in Cuba, Nixon snapped at once, 'I'd grab it.' I don't suppose that he shared the usual adolescent illusions about 'imperialism'.

In an essay on 'Mankind's Better Moments', Barbara Tuchman calls attention to the good side in the record, and gives us something of her credo. 'A study of history reminds us that mankind has its ups and downs, and during its ups has accomplished many brave and beautiful things, exerted stupendous endeavours, explored and conquered oceans and wilderness, achieved marvels of beauty in the creative arts and marvels of science and social progress', etc.

I never discussed these with her, and did not learn what she thought of my work on Shakespeare. I don't think she went into it, but probably kept an open mind about my Contemporary Shakespeare. The most generous of women, she gave a large party to launch it, at her home on the old Morgenthau estate at Cos Cob, on the coast of Connecticut. And she accompanied me when a New York School of Drama performed half-a-dozen scenes in my edition of Shakespeare's Plays, on the stage of Eugene O'Neill's little theatre in Greenwich Village. Her compatriot, Katherine Graham, however, confessed to an emotional attachment to disused 'thees and thous', which I do not share. And, a practising poet, I reflect that the archaic second personal singular necessitates the ugliest sound in the language, 'dst' – thou wouldst, shouldst, etc. – almost impossible for foreigners to pronounce when frequently followed by 'th', wouldst thou.

Tuchman cited some examples of creative enterprise through the ages, even one to raise our spirits in our disgraceful time. 'Consider how the Dutch accomplished the miracle of making land out of sea: by progressive enclosure of the Zuider Zee over the last sixty years, they have added half a million acres to their country, enlarging its area by 8 per cent, and providing homes, farms and towns for a quarter of a million people. The Zuider Zee was a tidal gulf penetrating eighty miles into the land over an area ten to thirty miles wide.' Now ...

Or consider the architectural explosion of the Gothic cathedrals of the Middle Ages. 'In a single century, from 1170 to 1270, 600 cathedrals and major churches were built in France alone.' In going round England with Pevsner in hand, I have been astonished by the architectural explosion – cathedrals, churches, monasteries, castles – which followed upon the Norman Conquest. She cites the extraordinary exploits of Viking seamanship – though here I am less impressed because of the destruction these marauders wrought. Or again she cites the epic discovery and exploration of the whole New World.

In our own time there is an even more wonderful achievement than that of the Dutch – the miraculous creation, or recreation, of the state of Israel. To this she devotes an eloquent essay, 'Israel: Land of Unlimited Impossibilities'. It is indeed all the more breathtaking for the obstacles and obstructions, the hostile forces and ever-present dangers, that this creative achievement has encountered. One of my few beliefs is in creative achievement, and I believed from the first that the Jews would make the desert blossom like the rose.

If there is any honour in all the world that I should like, it would be to be an honorary Jewish citizen. Since that cannot be, I can at least salute Barbara Tuchman as the leading woman historian of our time.

Index

205

Index

Index

Index